MY NEW NORMAL

MY NEW NORMAL

A Mother's Story of Love and Loss in the Opioid Epidemic

A MEMOIR BY

CHARLA BOCCHICCHIO

Better days with Cassidy, 2012

This book is dedicated to my angel, my only child Cassidy, and to the hundreds of other daughters, sons, friends, neighbors, parents, grandchildren and loved ones who are dying every day from this epidemic. My daughter is just one of the many, way too many. I miss her deeply and I know I can never have her back. This is my new normal. And it sucks!

Acknowledgments

First and foremost, I wish to express my gratitude and love to my adoring, supportive husband, John, for his encouragement and cheerleading throughout the process of writing and publishing this book. I am lucky to have had him by my side through this horrendous loss. Too numerous to name are the many family members, friends, colleagues and strangers that encouraged me to write about my experience. I also wish to thank my book designer and formatter, Claressa Swensen, for taking my hand and guiding me through this adventure as a first time author. Her expertise was so valuable. I also acknowledge and thank my amazing editor, Valerie Valentine. Her beautiful words of encouragement throughout the process, as well as her help in developing my story and recognizing my voice, helped me believe in myself as a writer. And finally, my love and gratitude to our Goldendoodle, Zoey for patiently listening to me ramble ideas on our walks and never judging me for bursting into tears on the neighborhood streets.

CONTENTS

PROLOGUE

A month after Cassidy died, I started feeling a tug. It began as one thought that grew into words strung together in my head, which was fueled by the constant pull from somewhere I couldn't see: *Write, write, write.* Like a child pulling at my sleeve, asking for attention ... *Mom, Mom, Mommy, MOM!! WRITE YOUR STORY!*

So I started writing. I didn't want to forget these feelings and memories. I realized very quickly that my relationship to Cassidy now only existed in flashbacks. Photographs helped, but the harsh realization that there would be no more photographs of her cut me like a knife.

Once I wrote about my first day without her, the rest seem to pour out of me. Now keep in mind, I have never written anything of note EVER! I hated writing in school because I felt like I wasn't any good at it. Turns out that I just needed something to write about. Something important. I found my story. Too bad it took losing my precious baby to find my purpose; but hey, we are all simply along for the ride on this rock circling the sun. And when we listen carefully with our ear to the ground, we hear *everything: the good, bad, the ugly, the beautiful, the light and even the darkness.*

I started to post my writings into a blog that I called *My New Normal.* I added blog posts to it for a year as my story continued to unfold, detailing my first year surviving the loss of my only child. I originally wrote for myself, because it felt good. It was cathartic and therapeutic to put into words the thoughts and emotions swimming in my head and through my heart.

What I didn't anticipate was how it would affect others.

It turns out that people really wanted to read about my experience. I was floored by the response I was getting. Some called it *raw, real, brave, important.* Other parents, grieving family members, friends, and complete strangers, all dealing with this epidemic on some level or another and from all over the world were reaching out to me to thank me for telling my story and putting into words what they were all feeling after losing someone they loved to addiction. So began my journey of writing this book.

And you are about to experience what it was like for me to survive the first year of this enormous loss. Tread lightly and maybe have tissues nearby, just in case.

CHAPTER 1

WHAT NO ONE TELLS YOU ABOUT LOSING A CHILD ... DAY ONE

My daughter died of a drug overdose. This is my truth now.

The morning of Friday, November 11, 2016, I woke up at my home in Salt Lake City, before my alarm went off to get ready for yoga. And as I always do first thing in the morning, I looked at my phone to see what I missed while asleep. The first thing that struck me was the multitude of missed calls from my ex-husband, Chris, in Birmingham, AL, starting at about three a.m. and continuing for hours.

I had started turning my phone to silent at night a few years ago so I could get sleep in the event that Cassidy might call or text from across the country in Alabama, where she was currently living, with some perceived catastrophe. It was a big step for me to create a boundary for myself, but in that moment, I was filled with worry and dread. A pit already growing heavy in my stomach.

Immediately, my heart raced. It would be a more normal occurrence to see that many missed calls from Cassidy, but not from Chris. Then I saw in my notifications the first line of a text message from him, which read like the beginning of an

obituary, "Cassidy Aspen Cochran was born June 22, 1994 ..."
I didn't dare open the full message. Instead, I jumped out of
bed and called him as I threw on my robe and walked quickly
downstairs, knowing in my heart this was the news I had feared
every day for the last several years, but hoping perhaps she was
just in the hospital or in jail.

As Chris answered the phone, I heard him utter the words
I couldn't bear to accept: "She's gone, Cassidy's gone, she's
dead, I'm so sorry ..."

I stopped listening after that and the only words that could
fall from my mouth were, "No, No, No," over and over and
over as I crumbled to the hardwood floor in the office next
to the kitchen. I sobbed and couldn't catch my breath, and
I couldn't even form real thoughts. It was as if my life had
stopped. Everything stopped. The only thing that remained
was the lump in my gut, the intense pain in my chest. I could
not accept this new truth, and I wasn't sure how to take my next
breath, let alone get off the phone with my ex-husband.

I managed to get the basic details: an overdose, heroin, with
Frank. He woke up, she didn't. Police at Chris's door at three
a.m. I can't remember what else. My mind just snapped shut. I
felt like I was floating above my body. Dreaming. *God, I would
give anything to wake up from this nightmare.*

As I walked back upstairs to wake my husband, John, I was
finishing the call with Chris. John was sitting up in bed, and as
he heard my goodbyes and heard me say to my ex-husband the
words "I love you, Chris, I'm so sorry," John knew.

He looked at me and asked, "When did it happen?"

After these first moments, there was a whirlwind. The tears,
the nonstop phone calls to family, the post on my Facebook
in an attempt to let everyone know at once, telling the awful
truth about how she died. Then the travel arrangements, more
tears, and a doctor visit for a temporary pharmaceutical fix to
reign in my new brain activity that made my body feel like it
would spin out of control if left unchecked. Falling apart in the
shower, laundry, packing for who knows how many nights in

a hotel in Birmingham. More tears and messages from friends and family, wondering, "What do I need to pack to attend my own daughter's funeral?" Then I might have remembered to eat, or maybe not.

CHAPTER 2

AND YOUR HEART GETS RIPPED FROM YOUR CHEST ...

Twenty-four hours after I heard the words, "Cassidy is dead," John and I were on an airplane headed to Birmingham, where I would identify my daughter's body later that afternoon. *This is what you cannot fathom until you live it.*

We touched down in BHM, where Chris picked us up to go straight to the funeral home to view the body. You see, the funeral director would only be there until five p.m., so time was of the essence.

Here's what happens: The funeral home is quiet, solemn even. The woman at the front desk is sweet, understanding, with that look in her eyes and expression on her face that becomes all too familiar in others during the coming days. The director has a soft voice and an accommodating attitude, although I am painfully aware that he actually has a family to get home to after we wrap up here.

Once Chris's brother and parents got there, we were all ready to go into a backroom where they had prepared Cassidy for us. Because she was going to be cremated, she was not embalmed. We all walked down a long hallway that felt never-ending and narrow. The longest hall I have ever walked, all the way, led to a single door. This doorway was most likely the hardest doorway I have ever walked through.

I crossed the threshold, and the only thing in the otherwise large room that I could focus on or even see, really, was a plain, makeshift little wooden "casket"—a box, really. A few steps further, I saw her. I saw her newly darkened hair, her pale beautiful face, a quilt covering her recently autopsied body, a white cotton gown, almost like a hospital gown, covering her shoulders. As I approached her, an unbearable and unstoppable rush of panic and sadness and anger and deep sorrow penetrated every cell inside of me.

I wailed, I cried out, I crumbled. "No, no, please, oh *God.* No, please no, my baby, oh, please no!" The only thing I wanted was for this all not to be true.

There was a part of me that was afraid to touch her. Chris said to trust him, that I needed to touch her. And once I did touch her, I didn't want to stop. Her skin was cold to the touch, but it was still her skin, soft; her hair felt as real and alive as ever, but her lips looked slightly chapped and a little more red than usual. There were moments when I fully expected Cassidy to open her eyes and start laughing hysterically at the ultimate practical joke she just pulled off. She simply looked like she was sleeping. I wanted nothing more than to pick her up out of that awful box and make her warm, to hold her tight and warm her body. Then the ache took over with the realization that it would be impossible.

We all stood around, awkwardly reminiscing and crying and laughing. Then the funeral director pulled me and Chris into the other room to sign the necessary papers and officially confirm that the body in the other room was indeed our baby. Everything about this was horrendous. It was too much to bear, and without the Xanax, I am convinced that I would have had a complete nervous breakdown.

After Chris and I signed the documents, we asked to go back one last time to say our goodbyes. The rest of the family was in the waiting room at this point. So the two of us alone, just as we started this journey twenty-two years ago, walked back into the room where our angel, our beautiful sunshine, lay sleeping and helpless, this time in a box, not a bassinet. We stood over her and caressed her skin and hair. We forgave each other for mistakes made long ago, and we tried the best we could to accept this new reality. We cried and we laughed; then, just as we did twenty-two years ago, we sang her a lullaby. The one Chris would sing to her as an infant when she was inconsolable. A slight variation on a Grateful Dead song. This was our goodbye to our baby, our only child, our everything:

"Lay down my dear sister, lay down and take your rest. Oh won't you lay your head on your daddy's chest. I love you, but your mama loves you the best and I bid you good night, good night, good night …"

Chris said his goodbyes with a kiss only a father could give. Then I fixed her hair by brushing it from off her forehead with my soft and trembling hand. I leaned down to kiss her forehead and cheek, and I told her goodbye and that I loved her for the last time.

I took a deep breath and walked out of the room, knowing that I would forever remember that moment and cherish it. This image of her … permanently imprinted on me … forever.

CHAPTER 3

ARRANGEMENTS

The most surreal moment is when you are sitting in a funeral home meeting room, making arrangements for your dead daughter, which happened the following day.

You're on autopilot those first few days. If I hadn't been dressing myself and brushing my own teeth for forty-plus years, I would have been lost that week ... Hell, I *was* lost, regardless of personal hygiene rituals. Sleeping was the thing that escaped me. It seemed the impossible task at that time, and I never had issues sleeping before. Once again, I was grateful for a little pharmaceutical help those first few weeks.

But mostly I was grateful for John, my husband of only a few short months at that point, newly thrust into the madness of this world I had been navigating for seven drug-addled years with Cassidy. He was stupendous! A kind, compassionate man with a gentle heart ... he ached, too. He mourned, too. He, like many others, had fallen under Cassidy's charming, intoxicating spell the first moment he met her. He hurt, too ... for her loss. And he hurt for me. He still hurts for me, as I don't know that I will ever stop hurting.

So there we sat, me, John, Chris (Cassidy's dad), Chris's girlfriend Stephanie, and Cassidy's boyfriend, Frank. Gathered around a board table at the funeral home, learning about all the nice, convenient services they could offer to ease our burden, to pad their pockets. The astounding thing to me was the price tag on all of this crap. This necessary and expensive shit that no one wants to think about at a time like this. You are completely at their mercy. We had agreed beforehand that we would do the cremation only, with no fancy urns, just get her cremains divided equally in two boxes: one for Mom, one for Dad. The plan was to spread her ashes in various places over the next year or so. Places she would have wanted to be. The beach, Disney World, southern Utah, a ski slope, NYC, perhaps backstage at the Alabama Theatre ... it all seemed so unimportant, yet at the same time, like some of the most important decisions I would ever make in my entire life. They asked did we want to be there when they cremated her body. I had no idea what I was supposed to do, and I never really answered. I said I would think about it. They showed us a video with options for memorial jewelry and services to remember your loved one. I was completely waterlogged at all of this, as I would continue to be for the weeks to come.

As we left the funeral home that day, everything was set in motion. We had signed papers that would approve the transfer of my baby girl's body to the crematorium downtown, where someone would push her into an oven in two days, where she would burn so hot that eventually she would be nothing but ashes. Ashes that I would carry home with me in a box.

This was my new normal.

CHAPTER 4

ASHES TO ASHES ... AND SURPRISING FACEBOOK NOTIFICATIONS

The night before Cassidy was to be cremated, I was seriously contemplating being there to experience all of it. Chris knew that he wanted to be and the plan was that we would meet at the crematorium the next morning. As the evening progressed, I felt myself getting more and more agitated. I wanted to crawl out of my skin and be on some other plane, watching it all from a safe distance. I knew I couldn't do it. I simply could not be there at the crematorium while my daughter was burned to ashes.

So ... I bailed.

And I have zero regret to this day about my decision. When Chris described the events later the next day to me, I could barely stand. I felt nauseous and dizzy. I was grateful he was there, and I'm not sure how he was able to handle it.

These are his words about that awful morning:

"We pulled around back.
In front of the crematorium.

They were waiting on us; the room was already prepared.
It was cold
Concrete.
Industrial.
Her makeshift "casket" was on a lift ... all alone in that cold,
empty, industrial room.
I couldn't breathe.
I walked over to her.
I lifted the casket and rolled it into the ... what do you call it?
Oven? Kiln?
I then slowly lowered the door.
I said, "Goodbye. I'm sorry."
I then pushed the button that started the fire.
I cried.
That was all I had left in me.

Twenty-two years before, I had been there as a witness
when Cassidy came into this world ... I saw her arrive, before
her first breath.

Twenty-two years later, I was there as a witness when
Cassidy's body returned to ash ... I saw her leave, after her
last breath was gone.

I can't explain the weight I felt at that moment. Everything I
had done wrong ... Every way I had failed her ... Every unkind
word said in anger or frustration ... fell upon me. Crushing me.
Pushing me to my knees.
It was done.
The act.
Not the pain."
- J. Chris Cochran

We all went the next day to pick up her ashes from the
crematorium. As we sat waiting in the quiet, somber foyer for
a woman to bring us our daughter in boxes, I felt a brick in my
chest. The gravity of this scenario is the heaviest I have ever
experienced. *It's surreal and it's horrible and it's the saddest
thing ever. Yet, it's really happening.*

Suddenly I heard my phone *bing* with a Facebook notification. I looked and it said something like, "You have been chosen as Cassidy Aspen Calzone's legacy contact. To manage her Facebook memorial profile, click here."

At first I mistakenly thought it was a message from Cassidy, which made me question my sanity. Then I realized that Facebook knew my daughter was dead and put into action her legacy contact plan. *What the ?!$# !*

This baffled me. How did they know? The timing of the Facebook notification was hysterical and ironic and sooooo Cassidy (as she was notorious for her ironic sense of humor and uncanny timing). Then the reality of what was happening at that moment in time started sinking back in. I was staring at my phone, sitting in a funeral parlor as a rotund woman rounded the corner with both hands full. She was carrying what looked like two large, insulated lunch bags with nice handles and the funeral home logo printed on the front. She softly handed them to me and said something about condolences, *blah, blah, blah*
...

So there we were: walking out of the crematorium carrying our daughter, split evenly between two boxes, now housed in fancy lunch bags. As we got to the rental car to put them in the back, I moved a box out of the way that had some of Cassidy's old keepsakes. I noticed a homemade, scrapbook-type book sticking out of the top, and I pulled it out to see what it was. There on the cover, in Cassidy's twelve-year-old handwriting were the words "BURN BOOK" (if you've seen *Mean Girls*, you will understand the reference).

As we stood in the parking lot, right next to the building where they literally burn bodies to ash ...

It took us about three seconds before we all found the irony and humor of that moment and started laughing hysterically.

This was the perfect ending to one horrific experience, and Cassidy would have *loved* it!

CHAPTER 5

HERTZ ... DON'T IT?

The rental car that John and I got at the airport in Birmingham was from Hertz. It was an upgrade, a midsized SUV, equipped with a GPS navigation device. Fancy! I think it was probably the second day driving it that John pointed out this cold realization: every time we started the car, she would announce loudly in her Siri-like voice, "Hertz."

... *Yes it does, thanks for the hourly reminder, every fricking time we start this ludicrous car, that my daughter is dead, and it hurts like hell each time I try to take a breath! Thank you so much for the ridiculous reminder, Hertz!*

As the week progressed, it seemed a constant and harsh, yet somehow friendly and pleasant-sounding reminder that taunted us: "Hertz ... Don't it?"

Note to self: we should have gone with Avis!

The day after Cassidy was burned to ashes, we had to attend to the task of planning her memorial service. We knew from the get-go that a traditional funeral in a funeral home or church simply would *not* do for Cassidy. After a few brainstorming sessions, the obvious choice came into focus. We would choose a celebration of life at a place that was a huge part of Cassidy's life: Children's Dance Foundation. Not only did I serve as their program director for sixteen years, starting when Cassidy was a toddler, but she really grew up there—in the hallways, studios, my office, the nooks and crannies of that wonderful, creative, magical place. This was the perfect venue to gather friends and family to remember her.

Without going into every boring detail of the arrangements, suffice it to say, I went into full production mode. This helped me tremendously! It gave me a purpose and something I knew well. My former colleagues at The Dance Foundation were amazing. They took care of everything for us in our time of need and made it simple, at no charge! I created the running order for the event, and I pulled together all the photos and music to be used for the video scrapbook that would serve as the living eulogy of Cassidy's short life.

It was all set in motion like a well-oiled machine. Everyone involved had a task or two. My "village" stepped up and made it happen.

I was so grateful!

The following day, my brother Derek and his wife LeEllen flew into town. Finally, my reinforcements; my posse; the cavalry. The only two from my side of the family who would travel from Utah to join me and John! I felt held up and supported in the most beautiful way once they touched down in Birmingham, Alabama. I somehow knew that we would make it through this horrendous week together. The wonderful thing about my brother and his wife is that we always have the best time together (the four of us), no matter the circumstances. That night, there was wine, food, laughter, and tears. But the thing that always remained was the constant tug at my heart, the weight of the situation, that shitty, gigantic rock in my stomach.

... Hurts, don't it?

CHAPTER 6

YOU'VE GOTTA DIE TO BE FAMOUS

In the weeks that followed Cassidy's death, her obituary, which honestly stated her cause of death, spread like wildfire on social media and online in general. Every time I would look at Facebook, I would see her photo (the photo I picked to accompany the obituary), over and over, along with some news source or addiction support group, or just an individual touched by our story, applauding us for the open, honest obituary. Chris wrote it in one draft in the hours after the police knocked on his door at three a.m. that fateful night with the bad news, before he could get through to me halfway across the country. I thought it was inspired then, and now I know it was.

When I would type "Cassidy Aspen Cochran" in the search bar on Facebook that week, it would say "30,000 people are talking about this." I did this more than I'd like to admit. Somehow it gave me comfort to know people were posting and sharing about my daughter. Like she hadn't just disappeared into thin air; she was still important to many.

There was a constant stream of messages, comments, and emails from complete strangers who had seen our story and wanted to reach out to say, "Thank you for being honest about how your daughter died." Or to say they had also lost a child to an overdose, or that they have a child in active addiction and wanted advice. This baffled me. I felt like the last person in the world they should come to for advice. After all, my daughter died. I failed. I couldn't save her. But, in reality, none of us can save our kids or anyone else when it is their time to go.

The ABC affiliate in Birmingham, ABC 33/40, contacted Chris and asked to do an interview with us about Cassidy's story that week. We said yes, and two days before her memorial service, Cynthia Gould and a cameraman came to the house to sit down with me and Chris, surrounded by piles of old family photos and keepsakes of Cassidy, to hear our story, see our tears, and look for answers.

After the story aired, Cassidy's story continued to go viral in the most amazing way. It is surreal, exciting, and heartbreaking to constantly see your daughter all over the Internet. Famous for … dying.

That was just the beginning. That original news story today has over half a million views just on the Facebook video version, which has been shared almost 7,000 times. To this day, we've done other TV news stories, interviews, articles and radio interviews about Cassidy's death, trying to raise awareness about Substance Use Disorder in an effort to stop the stigma of a disease that is killing a generation.

Coincidentally, or not, the week Cassidy died, the U.S. Surgeon General came out with a groundbreaking report stating, "Addiction is a chronic brain disease, not a moral failure." It was a call to action for citizens to address this public health epidemic that is "bigger than cancer." It seemed like the world was suddenly sitting up and paying attention.

Apparently, when a beautiful "girl next door" like Cassidy dies from a heroin and fentanyl overdose in suburbia, people do start to pay attention.

It took death for Cassidy to reach her true potential. We believed in her. She could have achieved anything she desired in this life. A song that become her theme song of sorts while she was in recovery, is called "Shine" by Anna Nalick. The beautiful chorus included this refrain: *We are all waiting on your supernova, cause that's who you are.*

Her whole life, it felt like we were waiting on Cassidy's supernova, but I don't think I understood what we were really asking for. Now I know ... and it's a bittersweet realization when you read the definition:

Supernova: an amazing and beautiful event that occurs during the last stellar evolutionary stages of a very bright star's life, whose dramatic and catastrophic destruction is marked by one final, titanic explosion. For a short time, this causes the sudden appearance of a new, even brighter light, before slowly fading over time.

Shine, sweet Cassidy! Everyone feels your light now. Now is when the world starts to change. People are starting to talk about addiction without shame. More and more obituaries are being written honestly and openly by families losing their children to overdoses. I can't help but think it's all because of you.

CASSIDY ASPEN COCHRAN
JUNE 22, 1994 – NOV 11, 2016

Cassidy Aspen Cochran was born on June 22, 1994. She was a precocious child. As soon as she could talk, she was quoting lines from Shakespeare. She loved to perform for friends and family. She called herself the "Queen of Make Believe." She was so smart, so funny. Even when times got tough, she could always make you laugh. She had a huge heart. She loved animals. All animals. Especially Harambe, the famous gorilla from the Cincinnati Zoo. Cassidy was so beautiful; stunning really. She recently had plans to marry her fiancé, Frank Calzone. She loved him and he loved her. She wanted to create a life with him. She seemed genuinely happy over the last year with him. Unfortunately, Cassidy also struggled with addiction. Her addiction finally won. She died of a heroin overdose in the early morning hours of November 11, 2016. We write this not to dishonor her memory but to shine some light on an illness that is taking the lives of far too many. If we allow shame, guilt or embarrassment to cause this illness to become a dark family secret, hiding in the shadows, everyone loses. Cassidy now joins the ever-expanding list of daughters, sons, sisters, brothers, and grandchildren taken far too soon by this growing healthcare epidemic. But, please remember, Cassidy isn't just a statistic, she was our sunshine, even when she kept us awake with worry. Everyone on that list was the light of someone's life. Thus, it is important to remember that Cassidy wasn't just her illness; she was our daughter and our friend. Words cannot describe how much she will be missed. Cassidy was preceded in death by her grandmother Frances Hale and her uncle Bradley "Boo" Cochran. She is survived by her fiancé, Frank Calzone, her father, Chris Cochran, her mother, Charla Hale Cochran Bocchicchio, her stepfather, John Bocchicchio, her grandparents, Tom and Barbara Cochran, her grandfather, Robert Hale and far too many aunts, uncles, and cousins to list. In lieu of flowers, please call or write your state representative and plead with them to make Naloxone (the powerful antidote for an opioid overdose) available over the counter, without a prescription.

CHAPTER 7

OMMMMMM …

My new normal since November 11, 2016 is that I am functioning at a fairly high level of anxiety most days. This is something I have never really encountered before on a regular basis. No one tells you about this phenomenon upon losing a child. It is a strange and alarming feeling. My hand will occasionally tremble when writing or applying mascara. At first I was terrified that I had Parkinson's disease, then my wonderful husband, John (who has dealt with anxiety most of his life) assured me that it was "just" anxiety. At times I feel like a motor is running on high inside my core. Not my heart, necessarily, but a revved-up, heightened energy deep inside me. Like I could jump out of my own skin.

Thankfully I had a temporary prescription to treat my "grief reaction," as they called it. I was most grateful for it at bedtime, as I knew full well there wasn't a snowball's chance in hell of my falling asleep without it during those early weeks. I simply couldn't turn my brain off. It broke my heart that Cassidy dealt with anxiety like this her whole life.

Now, you must know that I pride myself on my ability to stay calm under pressure. I have wonderful coping skills from my yoga practice and meditation. I have a small tattoo on my wrist that says the word "breathe." A Zen garden sits on my coffee table. I have studied all the Eastern philosophies and try to help others learn mindfulness. I have the whole Buddhist, Zen, calm thing down pat.

[Cue the laughter] *Bahahaha*, Mindful AF.

Apparently when one is pushed to their outer limit of human suffering, all bets are off.

So needless to say, I was kind of a wreck. Doing the best I could in each moment, knowing that I wouldn't feel like this forever. After all, everything is temporary.

[Cue the ugly snot crying] *Sigh.*

So, there we were, one of our nights at the Embassy Suites in Birmingham that first week. I had finally fallen asleep after an extremely emotional day (hell, every day was like that now), when out of the calmest slumber, came the loudest, most horrific noise on the planet. At three a.m., I was jolted awake to a high-pitched squawking of some kind of alarm in the hotel. So much confusion, noise, turmoil. At that moment, I felt like I was at war. All I could do was cry and scream out, "Why, why? Why is this happening?!"

As I sobbed there on the king-sized hotel bed, the alarm continued relentlessly. I was sure this was some attack on my sanity and a test! I felt utterly helpless. It felt like a bad joke. The universe's ultimate practical joke. And it was so *not* funny. John held me and tried to calm me down while also investigating whether or not we needed to evacuate the room.

As it turns out, our room was literally the only room in the hotel that was experiencing the alarm. *Ha*, maybe it was a cruel universe-joke. Actually, it was just our bathroom smoke alarm mistaking John's vaporizer vapor for smoke.

Well played, Universe!

CHAPTER 8

NOW WHAT?

We gathered that Friday, November 18, 2016 at The Dance Foundation in Homewood, Alabama to celebrate the short life of our daughter, friend, niece, grandchild, cousin, neighbor, student, classmate, stepdaughter, our sunshine, our Cassidy! Two news crew were there, too, following our story and getting footage to add to the interview they had already done with me and Chris a few days ago.

Looking back now, it seems like I was experiencing everything from behind foggy goggles. I remember it all in great detail, yet it would be more accurate to say that I was watching it all unfold from outside of myself.

We put on a great show that day for Cassidy. We were in the performance space at CDF, the place Cassidy had performed many times as a young actor and dancer. She had helped me with theatre camps and acting classes countless times, right there in that room. At the entrance of the space, we had set up a table with mementos and photos, bedazzled with feather boas, magic wands and fairy wings. Whimsical live piano pre-show music played from the grand piano, performed by an old friend and colleague, Steve McKinney. There were probably 250 or more chairs set up in the audience and at the front was an academic wooden podium draped with a purple boa, and next to it a trunk full of dress-up items for guests if they felt like playing. Front and center was a table adorned with colorful tapered candles and above it, a large screen that displayed a photo of Cassidy, one of her acting headshots taken in 2012. In it she is beautiful, blond, and full of promise, in a bright blue camisole top with the best smile ever. To this day, I can't look at that photo and *not* be immediately transported to that day. It has now come to represent the few hours our friends and family gathered to say goodbye.

The service itself was perfect. Chris and I both spoke. This is the eulogy I spoke about her as I stood in front of hundreds of loved ones that day and tried not to drown ...
We never intended to become the poster family for this

issue, but here we are. Cassidy died of a heroin overdose, this is our truth. We lived with this disease as a family for a very long time. We suffered, but not as much as Cassidy. For Cassidy, this disease was terminal. She has now been released. The reach of Cassidy's story is beyond our comprehension. As of this morning, over 40,000 people were "talking" about Cassidy Aspen Cochran on Facebook. Her obituary has been shared thousands of times by people from all over the country. Chris and I are getting messages and comments from hundreds of strangers every day, reaching out to comfort us and seeking comfort for their own situations. Local news stations are calling us for interviews. We are finding news stories about Cassidy all over the southeast. It is simply overwhelming ... and ... Cassidy would have loved this attention. But to many, she is just that photo on her obituary. To us, she was our daughter. To all of you, a granddaughter, a niece, a stepdaughter, a cousin, a friend, a neighbor, a student, a cast mate ... She was more than one photograph could ever capture.

Cassidy came into our world in the middle of the night twenty-two years ago, with a messy slip' n slide through a fountain of fluid, and eventually a gulp of air and a tiny cry. I wanted to feel everything, and as such we chose a natural, non-medicated birth at the freestanding birthing clinic in Salt Lake City, Utah. Chris and I were together every step of the way. From the moment we found out we were pregnant to the moment she breathed her first strong breath, we were there for her. She was our perfect little angel, and we were scared and ecstatic parents for the first and, as it would turn out, the only time. Cassidy Aspen Cochran burst into our lives on June 22, 1994 and immediately lit up the room. She has continued to do just that ever since.

Cassidy was a precocious and smart child. She did everything early! She walked at ten months, starting talking in complete sentences soon after, and she always seemed to have an old soul. Everyone saw it in her that knew us. Cassidy went with us wherever we went. She was with us always. Chris and I both worked with the University of Utah child abuse prevention program called TRUST. We toured together and toted Cassidy along in the back carrier to every show, sometimes handing her off to each other while one of us would go onstage to perform. She was included in our world always, surrounded by other adults and doted over by everyone who came in contact with her. She was adored by all, and she had the charisma, even at age one, to charm everyone she met. By about two and a half years old, she was quoting Shakespeare and performing for others every chance she got, finding her stage on a coffee table or the hearth of a fireplace. Anywhere she could be the center of attention to sing, act or dance for others. She shined bright! She dubbed herself the "Queen of Make-a-Beeve" and she ruled with grace (and a little bit of bossiness).

Before Cassidy turned three, I started teaching at Children's Dance Foundation and soon took over as Program Director. This became our second home and second family. Cassidy often came to work with me and found refuge and a wonderful fantasy world in the little, hidden storage area just above my office that we all termed the "Timeout Room." It was like a treehouse in the clouds to her, She would climb up the steps to that space with her fairy wings on her back and a fairy wand in her hand, and play for hours. Her imagination never ended. She started taking creative movement classes soon after and absolutely loved the freedom and creativity that brought. Her grandmother instilled a love of old movies and musicals in her from an early age, and she loved nothing more than to belt out show tunes for all to hear.

As she got older, she continued after my heart and passion for performing and acting. She was in many productions, mostly musicals, starting at age seven. She had the voice of someone twice her age and could belt with the best of them. She was a star. It seeped out of her like a billion bright lights that couldn't be contained. She was our sunshine.

She never quite fit the mold in school, and often we had frustrating calls from teachers. In third grade, I think her teacher believed she might have had some serious cognitive issues. But after a battery of tests, including IQ testing, the teacher and administration were dumbfounded to get the results that her IQ was in the triple digits and she was in fact way above average. We realized once again that we had a very special girl we were dealing with, and she required special attention. She struggled in a traditional school setting and started to show early signs of anxiety, among other issues.

She continued in theatre through her preteen years and excelled! But once she started middle school, social pressures weighed heavy, and she struggled with depression and anxiety. I remember when her friends reached out to me because they were worried about Cassidy, and this began a dialogue that, little did I know, would be the beginning of many more serious issues to come. I don't really want to rehash all the heartache and pain that Cassidy and this family experienced while she was a teenager and beyond. Just know that, at times, it was wrought with heartache, illness, hospital stays, depression and dysfunction. It was messy! And we still loved her. She used heroin for the first time at age fifteen. Chris and I did everything in our power to help her. We sent her to rehab, long-term treatment centers, therapy ... We never gave up on her. It took a toll on our jobs, our family, our whole world. And as you all know, it eventually took her life.

But Cassidy was so much more than her disorder, her disease. She was the life of the party, she was everyone's best friend. She was compassionate and kind. She was hilarious and irreverent and could literally make you laugh until you cried. She was talented and beautiful. She was charming and tortured and artistic and adventurous. She didn't care what people thought of her, and she loved practical jokes. She loved show tunes and trips to New York to see Broadway shows. She believed in magic and Harry Potter. She loved to snowboard and rock climb. We had a family tradition early on, as soon as she found out the truth about Santa Claus, that every Christmas, we would travel instead of doing Christmas at home. Some of my fondest memories of Cassidy are from our annual vacations at Christmas time: New York, Disney World, Universal Studios, Hawaii, Park City, Quebec, Whistler.

She went full throttle in everything she did. There was no halfway with Cassidy. In many ways, Cassidy and Chris were like playmates and would push every button of mine to get a laugh. She never stopped playing dress-up her whole life and never missed an opportunity to go to a Harry Potter premiere in her Gryffindor robe, carrying her wand. In retrospect, I think she always used make-believe as her escape from her inside pain. She had so many sides of her and could easily slide into any group and fit right in immediately.

Some of my favorite memories were road trips to the beach, singing at the top of our lungs to show tunes or other music favorites and harmonizing together. Chris gave it the old college try, but being a bit tone deaf, he usually deferred to me and Cassidy. Cassidy was in many ways my best friend, although recently we were separated geographically. And I miss her so much already. When Cassidy was at her best and healthiest, she was the brightest and most beautiful star in the night sky. She has now become her own supernova.

Cassidy always had a connection with and deep love of butterflies. To her (and to me) they came to symbolize her grandmother, my mother, who died of cancer eleven years ago this Monday. I always waited for Cassidy to emerge from her cocoon and to truly reach her potential in life. Because we all knew she could achieve anything she ever dreamed of. Truth is, she has now finally reached her potential, but it meant she truly had to leave behind her mortal body (her caterpillar).

"The caterpillar dies so the butterfly could be born. And, yet, the caterpillar lives in the butterfly and they are but one. So, when I die, it will be that I have been transformed from the caterpillar of earth to the butterfly of the universe."(-John Harricharan)

Cassidy is free now. She doesn't hurt anymore, she doesn't crave anymore, she left all her suffering and emerged with full

wings, a burst of light, an explosion of energy, to harmonize
with angels and surround us with pure, unconditional love.
    Cassidy, you are my Sunshine.

After I spoke, My brother Derek said a few words. An old
friend, Rosalind Litsey, and Chris's cousin Jenny said some
beautiful words as well. We played a song that a musician
friend of Cassidy had written about her in the last few days,
called "The Queen of Make-Believe." And then there was the
video scrapbook! A collection of photo memories and songs
that told our story, her story. During the last moments of the
video, the Grateful Dead song played, a live, a cappella version
of the song we sang to Cassidy as she lay in a box at the funeral
home, as the screen went to black and only her name appeared
in colorful lettering.

Immediately following the service, a playlist of music
started that we had put together to help everyone celebrate and
cry at the same time. Food was also available for guests, but
right away two long lines formed: one for me and one for Chris.
Many went through both lines. A multitude of familiar tear-
streaked faces, gazing at us sympathetically while in line, and
then outright sobbing once they got close enough to wrap their
arms around us.

This new normal was that I found myself consoling others,
offering sympathy for *their* loss. The loss of someone who was
important to them: my daughter. That's an odd realization and
feeling that would become all too familiar to me in the coming
months.

Eventually the lines dwindled and the crowd lessened to
mostly family, as staff members and wonderful friends started
cleaning up the mess and the leftovers; sweeping; stacking
chairs. At that moment, I felt an intense sense of sadness and
a tinge of anger. Here we all were, as always, cleaning up the
fucking mess that Cassidy always left in life. I was so mad at
her. She had always burst onto the scene, all drama and chaos
and love and laughter and jokes and sadness and anger, and in

her wake we were left scattered, the rest of us, in confusion and disarray. We'd shake our heads and ask ourselves, "What the hell just happened?"

Everyone was cleaning up the mess that night for *me*. I wasn't allowed to lift a finger. Perhaps this was my reconciliation. I was allowed to rest for a moment. I had earned it.

As we gathered the keepsakes, photos, flowers, guestbooks and other personal items to load into the cars, I knew this phase was over. The honeymoon of my grief was over. *Now is when the real work begins.*

... Shit is about to get real.

CHAPTER 9

SHIT DAY ... AND TSA AGENTS

I had survived without Cassidy for exactly one week! We lovingly dubbed November 11, 2016 as "Shit Day." Easier than referring to it as the day of Cassidy's death, I suppose, and funnier.

The arrangements had been carried out, the service was complete. Closure, right? ... Ummm, not so much.

We spent two more days in Birmingham before coming back to the reality of home. Thank God our bodies have a protection mechanism in that first week. It's like there is a soft-focus filter on everything, in addition to the immense amounts of love from others and a steady stream of condolences. We are held up, wrapped in kindness, bathed in the soothing salve of the love of others. Then we go home and are left to sit in our pain, our loss. Alone.

The day John and I flew back to Salt Lake City, was a somber day. In a week, we had gained several boxes full of Cassidy's belongings and keepsakes to take back with us, in addition to the insulated "lunch bag" from the funeral home that housed the box full of Cassidy's ashes. My new normal that day was that as I packed my toiletries in my luggage and made room for other last-minute items, I also tucked this container into my carry-on bag, along with a certificate that would allow me to fly on a plane with my daughter in a small box.

When we got to the airport and reached security, I suddenly realized that there would be a need to tell one of the TSA agents that I was carrying Cassidy's cremains. This is another thing that boggled my mind ... how could I be forty-eight years old and never have heard the term "cremains" before?

I digress.

The scene: John and I are taking our shoes off and loading our belongings into bins to push onto the conveyor belt through the x-ray device. I am trying to get the attention of one of the agents standing by as I place my carry-on bag onto the belt. "Excuse me ... I need to tell someone that I am traveling with my daughter's cremains and I have this certificate right here."

The uniformed woman nonchalantly responds, "Oh honey, they'll figure it out on the other side."

I start to worry. "But don't they need to know *now*?" ... No response.

John and I nervously stand on the other side of security now, getting our shoes back on and waiting for our other bags to pass through. Our eyes steadily focus on the agent checking the x-ray monitor as my carry-on bag slides underneath and ... *stops*! The agent does a double take.

I try to get her attention, rambling, "I have the certificate right here. I am traveling with my daughter's cremains ... *blah, and blah de blah* ..." It's almost as if I am invisible.

At that moment, the agent grabs the bag off the belt and motions to other agents. "I need a bag check over here."

At least three of the TSA's best and biggest agents walk over as another man gives an order, "We need a dye test over here!"

John and I are speechless as they get to work. It is surreal and confusing as I am standing there on the other side of a Plexiglas barrier, holding the certificate up so they know what is in the box. I could have been holding a letter from Barack Obama and no one would have cared. Procedure is procedure, and this was going down no matter what. The man gets to work with the dye test, rubbing a special paper along the seams of the box, then another, then dropping liquid onto the paper from a dropper ... as the TSA Thug Squad stands by.

John and I are getting a little teary as all this goes down.

Finally they complete their procedures and send us on our way with their condolences, after verifying that there was nothing more than a dead daughter in that box. Just like I told them from the beginning.

As John and I gathered everything up to continue on to our gate, he starts chuckling and then stops and says, "You know, the fact that at least five TSA agents thought for a moment that Cassidy's ashes *could* have actually been a kilo of cocaine ... is *hilarious!*"

And he was absolutely right. Cassidy would have laughed her ass off. That was the kind of moment that she would have relived and retold over and over, and it would have gotten funnier every time.

As I wiped my laughter tears from my cheeks, they mixed with my sadness tears. I took a deep breath and off we went, pulling our wheeled carry-on bags down the *terminal* where we would board a plane for SLC.

Home ... where everything would be different now.

CHAPTER 10

ON THE CORNER OF ANGER AND FORGIVENESS

The day John and I flew back to Salt Lake City from Birmingham happened to also be the eleven-year anniversary of my mom's death. It felt like God, the universe, or whatever you want to call It, was screaming out to me, "I'm not finished with you yet, *and* I want you to feel everything until I am."

I was exhausted ... Uncle, already! I wasn't quite sure how I was supposed to navigate life without Cassidy now. Strange, because I had been living away from her for nearly three years by this time. In 2012, Cassidy and I moved to Los Angeles together for acting opportunities. A couple years later, when Cassidy was once again spiraling out of control and had managed to sabotage any hope of a successful acting/modeling career, she moved back to Birmingham to be closer to her dad as well as a better recovery network (at least that was the hope). Not long after that, John and I decided to move to Utah in hopes of a simpler, less costly life   outside of Southern California. But just because there was distance between me and Cassidy, didn't mean it was easy for me to create healthy boundaries with her. By some miracle, I had finally reached a point where

I could fall asleep at night and not worry every second where she was. I had learned to let go more than ever before in my life. I loved her immensely *and* I was able to accept that she was an adult and culpable for her own decisions. I had no control over her day-to-day life anymore.

When I came back to my regular daily activities in Salt Lake that week, it was incredibly easy to just forget that anything devastating had even happened. Other than the laminated bookmark of Cassidy's obituary on my fridge and the few boxes of mementoes I had yet to go through from Birmingham, nothing had changed ... really.

Except for the fact that I now slept with Cassidy in a box next to my bed, and that I had to take a sleep-aid at night, and that every time I went to sleep I prayed that I could dream about her, just to feel her with me once again.

I felt abandoned. I had always heard these beautiful stories of loved ones who had passed on, reaching out to make contact beyond the grave with those left behind. Speaking to them in a dream, showing themselves in some other ways, as a butterfly, or a song heard on the radio, a message from them somehow. Yet from Cassidy, my own flesh and blood, I got nothing! What am I, chopped liver? This made me feel angry, frustrated and so alone. I believed that I deserved to hear from her. *Now!*

One morning, I was awakened by a loud crash from somewhere in the bathroom. As we pulled ourselves out of bed to see what the hubbub was about, we saw that the floor-to-ceiling shower caddy had somehow (inconceivably) fallen over in the shower and landed with a crash, dumping shampoos, conditioners and body wash all over the shower floor.

Okay, this had never happened before and seemed impossible, really. We immediately blamed Cassidy for the mishap and had a good laugh (secretly, I wished she had written in secret letters on the glass shower door, which would only appear when the steam fogged up the room).

That same morning, Rachel, John's oldest daughter who lived with us, recounted events from the previous day. She explained that she had twice found herself locked out of her bathroom downstairs (an event that had never happened to her before)! There was simply no other explanation! Cassidy had stayed in that bedroom two years previous when she came for a visit at Thanksgiving, before Rachel moved in with us. Another paranormal event that could only be explained by Cassidy!

I wanted more! I toyed around with the idea of going to see a medium (an idea that John wasn't crazy about and one I let go of after more consideration). Then one morning, Chris sent John a Facebook message explaining that he had clearly received a "message" that night in a dream from Cassidy. It was for *me*. Why my ex-husband was messaging my now-husband after meeting each other for the first time to view our dead daughter, instead of messaging me directly, was beyond me. In any case, this is what he relayed:

Chris's message to John:

I just woke from a dream. I got a message from Cassidy's energy—it's confusing to try and explain. The message was specifically for Charla. This is exactly what (let's just call it Cassidy) said. She said, "Mom is really worried whether I'm safe and okay and really free from pain." She then said to tell Mom that, finally, this isn't about her. She then laughed (inside joke, I guess?). She then said, "Don't worry, love saves everyone in the end—everyone—that saving love (that energy) is inside you and surrounding you now." She said to also tell her to stop blaming herself, there was no combination of words or hugs that could have saved her from the pain she was running from, but that Mom's love, your love and the love of all those who know how to love, burns away all the fear and all the pain in the final moment and leaves perfect Peace and Contentment in the ashes. She said to also tell her that it is okay to be okay, we've all suffered enough already. She said to say the last part twice. "The time to heal is now and this now has never existed before. Embrace it and breathe it in." She couldn't explain more ... Apparently words don't exist to describe it ... She laughed again and then said, "You know this isn't really ME me, this, this is all you, it's where I live now. Love lives in you. Love lives inside Mom."

... And that was it. When John showed me the message I was floored. I couldn't stop the tears from flowing. This was the message I had yearned for, wanted more than anything. *And* I was pissed! Why couldn't she just come directly to me? I couldn't help but feel resentment that I got a secondhand (actually third-hand message) from my own daughter. She came out of my body, while I remained completely unmedicated, I might add, and yet she couldn't just come directly to me to tell me this beautiful message from the other side? Why? Why didn't I deserve that respect? I was baffled, confused, sad, angry, and grateful at the same time.

It was just what I needed. And I wanted more. I knew dreams held the key, so I slept more than I probably should, and still—nothing.

As I marinated in these confusing feelings, I realized that perhaps she would only come to me directly when I was really ready.

Shit! ... Okay, Universe, message received loud and clear.

Apparently there is still some manner of internal garbage that I have yet to deal with before affording myself the luxury of intra-dimensional messages from loved ones on the other side. *Sigh* ...

I think I may start looking for clarity tomorrow, on the corner of anger and forgiveness.

CHAPTER 11

CASSIDY'S STORY, ACCORDING TO CASSIDY ...

I found a school paper of Cassidy's on my laptop just a few weeks after her death. I think it's such an interesting look at her life, according to her, as a teenager. It's a heartbreaking peek into the mind of an addict and the perceptions of a brain that had been remapped by opiates. Most of all, though, I hear the hope she had! She could have achieved *anything!*

This narrative that she tells of herself in third person is only a tiny fraction of her story as a whole. There was also a lot of love, forgiveness, second chances, and laughter in our home as she grew up. Honestly, her underlying issues (depression, anxiety, personality disorders) made it difficult for her to see the positives. So instead, she latched on to a narrative of never-ending pain and sadness. I know now that she understood we were doing the best we could with the tools we had, and I also know that she understood that we love her very much!

The following was written by seventeen-year-old Cassidy Cochran in 2011 for her English 12 class assignment.

Cassidy's Story, So Far ...

It all started around midnight, June 22, 1994, in Salt Lake City, Utah. These two hippies were at a local birthing center, having a little girl that would be named Cassidy Aspen Cochran. Cassidy and her mom Charla were on a welfare medical program; times were rough, money-wise.

Sometime in 1995, Cassidy's father, Chris, got accepted to the law school of his choice back home in Birmingham, Alabama. So off the little Cochran family went!

Cassidy's home life as a child was very chaotic. There was a lot of fighting and dysfunction. Her OCD (Obsessive-Compulsive Disorder) came to be obvious around her preschool years. It looked as though Cassidy had no control over anything, not even being loved in the proper way, so she tried to hang on to any sort of pattern of behavior that she could. In these years, young Cassidy felt alone. She couldn't connect with other kids. Other kids were happy and free while she was trapped in a broken home where her parents weren't emotionally available to love her enough. On a brighter note, around this age, also a little earlier, she began to perform Shakespeare and *Les Misérables* for her family. When she acted or sang, she felt important and worthy. This gave the young child purpose.

At age six, Cassidy got her first role in the play, *A Tale of Two Cities*. She fell in love. Acting was what she wanted to do forever. By the age of about ten, she had already been in ten musical theatre productions. This was her passion. In the hidden backstage of her life, her parents had gotten divorced, and her dad was spiraling out of control in his addiction. He went to rehab for three months. Family life got a lot better. The scars weren't all the way healed. It's hard to even understand resentments as an eight-year-old. While all of this was going on, Cassidy had to grow up a lot in order to assume these adult responsibilities that were required of her to help her dad and her mom. She wasn't able to be a child from that point on; she had seen too much already.

In Cassidy's middle school years, things got rough. She

began physical fights at school, smoking weed, popping pills, drinking alcohol, and cutting herself all in those three years. Her life got very dark and hopeless in her eyes. Older kids would tell her to kill herself. What they didn't know was, she was already planning on it. By the end of the eighth grade, she went into a psychiatric unit for attempts at suicide.

Cassidy began high school as an alcoholic with a drug addiction. All of her friends were upperclassmen. That year she found this church group called "The Basement" that she was convinced changed her life. She became outwardly *obsessed* with church and thought she'd never use drugs or drink again. She eventually used and drank again and again and wondered why. She eventually gave up on the church phase and moved on to a codependent relationship. The boy didn't approve of drugs, so she stayed clean from drugs and would only drink occasionally. It could be controlled, but only for a short period of time. After their messy breakup, she ended up diving headfirst back into her drug use, and within a matter of days she was smoking crack cocaine and mixing it with benzodiazepines. Before long she was heavily using cocaine, OxyContin, Ecstasy and Xanax. Not long after that, she began selling Ecstasy.

A boy came into her life; he was in a gang and he wanted her. She wanted him, and they "fell in love." Cassidy got the idea to start injecting cocaine into her veins because her nose was in horrible shape and she wanted a better high. She found it. She and her boyfriend bonded over their shared IV drug use. Only three days after Cassidy's sixteenth birthday, she had a seizure from injecting bricked cocaine mixed with methamphetamine. Her seizure was short-lasting, she came out of it and was okay, just had a slight headache. This was not a big enough warning for the two, apparently, because only fifteen minutes later, the boyfriend went into a full-out grand mal seizure, choking and not breathing. She was on the phone with 911 immediately. They decided to quit.

They stayed clean from cocaine for only a few days, the

whole time using Xanax and alcohol heavily. Then one day, a new drug dealer gave them a free bag of heroin to try. After that, cocaine came back and heroin was introduced into their lives through their veins. Shooting heroin every second of every day was how Cassidy lived. Eventually, she did way too much. she stopped breathing and her heart stopped beating. She was dead for approximately ten minutes. Her boyfriend gave her CPR for a long time, luckily starting her heart back up. He never dialed 911. Cassidy was injecting heroin again only thirty minutes later. This dark winding road led her to rehab eventually.

After her struggle with staying sober for nearly two years, she finally now has over a month sober. Cassidy stays sober today first and foremost for herself, her family, and her career. After initially getting clean, she was discovered by a talent manager based in L.A. Once she had gotten cleaned up again for a few weeks the second time, now feeling a lot different and ready, she went out to Los Angeles with her manager and got signed by an agency! Her career has been her dream since she could talk!

Her main focuses today are her sobriety: working with a sponsor, going to meetings, and helping other recovering addicts. Her career means staying on top of her public image, constant communication with her manager and agent, and making moving arrangements from Birmingham, Alabama to Los Angeles. And last but not least her family; she spends time with them every night before bed and as much time as possible with their busy schedules, and they have positive communication together!

If others and Cassidy herself had to describe her today, they'd say: confident, somewhat insecure, humble, video gamer in her spare time, loves to sleep, Dead Head, absolute animal lover, stubborn, opinionated, passionate, constantly changing laugh, huge-hearted, vegetarian, slightly shoe-obsessed, not religious– strictly spiritual, hilarious, intense, impulsive, an old soul, charismatic, intelligent, beautiful, butterfly whisperer,

tree hugger, ever-changing and always growing.
THE END

Cassidy, age sixteen, playing in the rain after a service
project for her residential treatment center in Southern Utah,
2011

CHAPTER 12

HAS ANYONE SEEN MY ZEN?

I knew my first day back to yoga (post-Shit Day) would be emotional, hard, wonderful and very much needed. I was craving it and afraid of it at the same time. That fateful morning a couple weeks ago, when I heard that Cassidy was dead, one of the first phone calls I made was to my yoga instructor, Dana. After all, it was a Friday and she would have expected me. I needed to tell her what had happened. I needed her to know.

So here I was, returning after two weeks of actively grieving the death of my only daughter, my only child, the only baby that had grown in my sacred belly. As I entered the studio, I immediately felt at ease *and* anxious. Everyone gave me space, and as I gathered my props and laid out my mat, my old comfortable ritual had begun. Hugs were abundant at first. Then we quieted ourselves and practiced.

As we gathered ourselves onto our mats, sitting upright, closing our eyes (I think I kept mine open on Dana's suggestion), we took a deep breath, chanted *ohm*, and so it began.

I first realized there would be a problem when we made a brief stop in child's pose after downward-facing dog, as usual. You see,

Cassidy was found in the wee hours on November 11, downward facing, on her knees with her head on the ground (child's pose). That's how she died. That is the image I had burned in my brain. I wondered then if I would ever be able to do child's pose again. Turns out that one day, much later, I would, and more importantly, I would eventually find solace there, while always making the connection to that image. But for today—not so much.

Dana kept an alert and compassionate eye on me that morning during our practice, and for the most part it was just what I needed, both physically and spiritually. I was proud of myself for holding it together so well and not running in tears from the studio. As we finally settled into what would become our savasana at the end of class, it began. Every emotion that had reared its head over the last two weeks—sadness, loss, anger, frustration, emptiness, you name it—was bubbling deep inside me as I tried to breathe and let go into "corpse pose."

Finally, after about five to seven minutes, Dana started to chant softly and very slowly (as she often did to bring us out of savasana), but this time it felt different. It was a slight variation on her usual chant. It was a beautiful tune, and the Sanskrit words covered me like a blanket this time. As her chant continued, I was convinced I heard more than just her voice. The studio was suddenly filled with a multitude of the most amazing, soulful, angelic voices I had ever experienced. I heard so many sounds, so many voices. And then it stopped with an echo ... as we came out of our final resting pose to an upright seated position before opening our eyes. My eyes were already slippery with tears. I was overwhelmed with feeling. Complete mush. Then after attempting to join the others with my broken voice, in the final three *ohms*, I bowed my head, rested my hands on my thighs, lifted my heavy head and slowly opened my wet eyes.

As I looked around the room, I realized that I was not the only one in tears. All these beautiful, compassionate women had joined me in my grief at that moment. Communal grieving at its best. I felt the most complete and intense love in that moment, and I was overwhelmed with gratitude. Dana asked everyone to gather close around me as they presented me with the most thoughtful and sweet gifts from the class, my fellow yogis. I was dumbfounded, happy, touched, and oh so grateful. Among other items, they gifted me a certificate for a massage at a local Japanese-style spa. I couldn't wait for that!

So, with a tear-streaked face and a gentle smile across my lips, I gathered my things and exited the yoga studio for the drive home, alone with my heavy thoughts. Yoga would continue to heal me. I was sure of that.

Namaste ...

CHAPTER 13

OH, PLEASE DON'T ASK ...

It had been one month since Cassidy's death, and I had already gotten back to work. I had several auditions, gave private coaching sessions and was acting in three different projects: a commercial, a short film and a public service announcement. It felt good to be busy—less time to ruminate and get stuck with own thoughts. The outside world seemed a much safer place lately than the dark, quiet corridors of my mind. And after all, I knew that Christmas was around the corner, so chances were those unsettling hallways up there were bound to get pretty crowded with thoughts of regret, sadness, anger and despair. At this point in time, I much preferred fantasy land.

The short film I was shooting was called "The Art of Dying," and I happened to be playing the role of a mother of a young woman who *dies*. Yes, you read that right. A little close to home much? The PSA that I booked was for an organization called How We Die. I know, right? Okay, Universe, once again, I get it. There would be no escaping those dark recesses of my inner self. Duly noted.

So after crying my eyes out on set for "The Art of Dying," in a scene where I find a note from my deceased daughter, left behind for the family to read, I figured I could handle anything!

I kind of think I was right, now that I look back. The cast and crew on that shoot were very sensitive to my situation, and they all knew about what had happened to Cassidy. I was handled delicately and I very much appreciated it. In fact, the director asked my permission to dedicate the film in Cassidy's memory. I was deeply touched and grateful.

When it came time to shoot the PSA spot, I had a different experience entirely. No one on that set knew about the events I had gone through in the last month, unless they had stalked my Facebook page. Which, I realize now, was quite possible and more likely even probable. Rephrase -*to my knowledge*, none of the cast and crew knew about what had happened on November 11, 2016.

I showed up early as usual, and I was the first one in hair and make-up. I tried to keep conversation light and small. Then the other cast members arrived: the actor playing my husband and the actress that would play my mother. So we were all in the same room as I sat in the make-up chair. The other two actors struck up a conversation that I noticed slowly turned to the subject of family. It went something like this (or more accurately, *this* was how my brain heard it):

"So, do you have kids?"

"Yeah, I have two. They are great. Straight-A students, soccer team captain and head cheerleader. Youngest just got accepted to Harvard and the oldest will be joining the Peace Corps next year. So proud of them."

"That's wonderful!"

"And what about you? Do you have children?"

"Oh yes, three children. I couldn't be prouder. They are all grown now and have kids of their own. I became a grandmother for the fourth time this year. My oldest is a brain surgeon, the second is an attorney and my youngest is married to the head of a university. They all live in multimillion-dollar estates and vacation in Bali every year."

I sit with my eyes closed as the make-up artist is carefully applying eye shadow, and I am quietly listening to this exchange, but *this* is what my brain activity actually sounds like:

"Oh shit, I have to get out of here. I'm next. They are going to ask me next! What do I say? What's the right answer? How do I respond to that question now? These people don't know me, and I don't want to burden them with such a big downer. Here, let me drop this big old doozy on everyone after this pleasant and positive exchange you were having about your wonder-children. What would I say? ... Oh, yeah, I had a daughter, umm, I guess I still have one? Anyway, yeah, she died a month ago. Umm, it was a drug overdose. Yeah, oh it's fine, I'm okay, really. Oh, she died on her bathroom floor with a heroin needle stuck in her arm."

... Mic drop.

Okay, so here's what really happened:

Me: "Oh boy, I really have to use the bathroom, are you done with my make-up?" as I bolted for the bathroom before they could ask me *The Question.*

I hurried into the hallway bathroom and locked the door behind me. This is when the tears started welling up. *Damn it, I just had my make-up done. Pull yourself together, Charla!* So I did. Of course, I had to stay in there long enough so they would have changed the subject by the time I got back out there. And once I reemerged, all was well. No one was the wiser.

So, even to this day, I find myself still wondering, how do I answer that question? It's bound to happen again. Hell, if I'm being honest, I never liked that question, even when Cassidy was alive. Everyone always bragging about their stellar, overachieving children, and then I would try to be vague when talking about my only child so no one would know that I raised a heroin addict. Now, I am ashamed of myself for allowing that stigma to affect me that way. No more, I say!

This is me now. I am shouting from the rooftops.

MY ONLY CHILD, MY AMAZING CASSIDY, SUFFERED FROM SUBSTANCE USE DISORDER. IT TOOK HER LIFE. AND I STILL LOVE HER! SHE WAS BEAUTIFUL INSIDE AND OUT, AND SHE TRULY KNEW

HOW TO LOVE! SHE LIVED FIERCELY AND WAS THE BRIGHTEST STAR IN MY GALAXY. I AM LUCKY TO HAVE HAD A DAUGHTER LIKE HER! SHE TAUGHT ME HOW TO SURVIVE, HOW TO LIVE FULLY AND HOW TO LOVE!

... echo, echo, echo...

CHAPTER 14

AND, THE MOTHER OF THE YEAR AWARD GOES TO ...

When someone we love dies, we tend to focus only on the good in them. I would go so far as to say that we might even lift them up to saint status at times. After all, turning them into an angel is much easier than remembering the hellish reality their life was from time to time. To be clear, I understand that Cassidy's occasionally unbearable behavior was almost always a byproduct of her disease.

However, I still wanted to strangle her sometimes for acting like such a little shit. As you might suspect from this admission, I was not exactly the Mother of the Year! Hell, if I'm being honest, I was never even a contestant. And that's really hard for me to admit.

Let me try to explain just what it's like to love someone who suffers from Opiate Use Disorder. As an added bonus, Cassidy also suffered from generalized anxiety, depression, and at age eighteen received a diagnosis of Borderline Personality Disorder. That's a doozy when it comes to treatment, and it's a disorder that almost always goes along with addiction.

So let me rephrase: Let me try to explain what it was

like living with and loving *my daughter*, Cassidy. She felt everything! I repeat—*everything*! Perhaps a little more than most. When she was happy, she was ecstatic! When she was angry, she was a monster. And when she was sad, she wanted to die. This was her life.

Let's start with the good news: she was a beautiful girl, stunning really. She was wicked smart and had the sharp mind of one much beyond her years. Her sense of humor was irreverent, quick, persistent, and hilarious. She had the wise, knowing eyes of an old soul and the kind, compassionate heart of angel. Her wide-open and infectious laughter could cure anything—except her own disease. When she was at her healthiest, she was the brightest star in the galaxy. Her light could shine for miles with vibrancy, laughter, and love. So how could there be any bad news about a girl like that? You might ask ...

Well, let me tell you. When Cassidy was at her worst and in the darkest depths of her disease, she could be unbearable. She was the world's best liar. She could manipulate the Buddha to get what she wanted or needed. And when she was craving, all bets were off. It was as if someone came in the middle of the night and replaced my sweet daughter with a demon that looked just like her. She would steal, lie, call us names, say hurtful, horrible things, throw things, break the law if necessary, threaten to hurt herself (at times wielding a butcher knife), cut herself. And at least one of those behaviors, or more likely a steady barrage of a combination of them, would eventually work its magic on me, and I would succumb to her demand of the day, whatever it was, just to keep my own sanity and keep her alive (so I thought) ...

Boy, was I wrong. I became the world's best enabler. Of course I didn't see this at the time. And honestly, that is one of the things that haunts me. My own less-than-stellar behavior. Maybe if I could have done something differently, I could have saved her. Oh, the familiar cry of the parent who has lost a child to an overdose ... I realize now that is utter nonsense.

However, there is one thought that will always haunt me. And if I'm not mistaken, it's a thought that other bereaved parents, in similar circumstances, have also had when their child suffering from SUD was still alive. But no one likes to admit it because it sounds horrendous. "Worst parent ever" kind of stuff. Here's your warning: this is not pretty. It will sound horrifying and awful, and maybe I was the world's worst mother and overall bad person for thinking it. But here goes:

There were times during Cassidy's lowest moments in her life when I actually thought it would be better if she just died.

Okay, so after you process that and gain your bearings enough to keep reading, I will explain ... I'll wait ... take your time ... breathe ... please try not to hate me or judge me too harshly.

Are you still with me?

Okay: Let me explain.

One doesn't get to that point easily. And it's not even a consistent thought. It comes and goes like the wind, and you never pay much attention to it. Until that day you get the phone call or the police knock on your door to tell you that your daughter really did die.

Then you are riddled with guilt as you fixate on that one thought, and it makes you physically sick, now that she's really gone. You can't stop thinking about the times you said it to yourself silently. *Did I wish this into reality? Did God answer a halfway uttered prayer I made in desperation one night while I watched Cassidy self-destruct?* The hardest thing to come to terms with now is that in some ways, it actually *is* better for her not to be alive.

Okay, stay with me on this ... some of her suffering that contributed to that unthinkable thought included the following:

• Cassidy's multiple suicide attempts and subsequent stays in hospital psychiatric units since about the age of thirteen.

• Getting a phone call from her boyfriend that she was rushed by ambulance to the hospital after cutting her arteries in her arms wide open. And then seeing her there bleeding, still combative and angry enough to need restraints in the ER before they could staple her together.

• Her constant physical suffering when craving that damned heroin.

• Her recurring state of crisis with relationships and boyfriends, including physical and emotional abuse from them.

• Her many hospital stays after contracting Hepatitis C from an infected needle.

• More ER visits than I could possibly count for a multitude of reasons, both physical and emotional.

• So many episodes of emotional distress that I eventually became numb to them, including: cutting herself repeatedly, almost always needing stitches, holding a knife to her own throat, threatening to kill herself, taking so many pills that her stomach needed pumping, running away, calling the police on her dad when he tried to wrestle a knife away from her, calling me at work in the middle of the day, threatening to slit her throat and write in her own blood on my bedroom wall that it was my fault ... the list goes on.

Please understand, I don't say these things to vilify Cassidy. I understand that she was a victim of her disorders. She was suffering, much like a stage-four cancer patient. *That* is where the unspeakable thought comes into play. As a parent, you can only watch your child suffer for so long before it occurs to you that things might be better if they could be put out of their misery, to be released from their otherwise unstoppable pain.

I remember feeling that same way when watching my mother suffer from cancer eleven years earlier. It's a heart-wrenching experience, to sit by helplessly and watch someone you love writhe in pain, thrash about with absolute despair and agony, and cry when waking to realize they didn't die in their sleep that night. I didn't feel guilty about praying those nights that my mother would be taken swiftly and mercifully so she wouldn't have to suffer anymore. I also didn't feel guilty for the feeling of great relief I experienced the day she finally did go. It was a blessing, a gift, that she could be released from her cancer-riddled earth-suit in exchange for eternal bliss.

So here I sit, trying *not* to feel guilty that I actually feel an ounce of relief that Cassidy is no longer suffering in *her* earth-suit. Believing that she has left behind all the turmoil of her mortal diseases. She is free now. I have to cut myself some slack for praying that Cassidy would be released back then, that she might be free of her pain. If I'm being totally honest, I wanted to be free of it, too. I wished to be free of the suffering that her disease was causing me, our family. We all suffered enough for too long.

And with that realization I am choosing now to try and forgive myself. I have to forgive myself for having those thoughts when she was still alive. I must give myself permission to have wished my only daughter wouldn't suffer anymore. And with that self-forgiveness, an amazing realization washes over me ... *That* seems to hold the magic key to forgiving Cassidy. She didn't choose any of this for herself. She did the best she could with what she had here on Earth, with two imperfect parents who loved her wildly through it all.

I was the best mother I could be with what I had in front of me, *and* I certainly wasn't perfect. I made so many mistakes. The only constant was that I loved Cassidy with every piece of me, and I wanted her to be truly happy, and to know how much she was loved. I'm pretty sure she knows now. And that makes it somehow all worthwhile, despite the suffering. Perhaps she did have a life worth living. Rephrase: I *know* she did. After all, she taught *me* how to love and how to forgive, and that is a beautiful lesson.

So ... if it's still up for grabs, I think I would like to accept that Mother of the Year Award now.

CHAPTER 15

STAGE TWO: ANGER

I get so mad at her sometimes! It usually happens when I'm scrolling through Facebook and a photo of Cassidy pops up, all smiles and silliness or that striking, stunning beauty she possessed.

... Ughhh. It's like the weirdest combination of emotions. Part of me wants to pick up the phone and call her. Another part wants to gaze into her hazel eyes forever and get lost in memories as nostalgic tears roll down my cheeks, and yet another part of me wants to throw my laptop through a window and destroy every photo of her I can find so I won't ever have to miss that face again!

Okay, perhaps not the healthiest way to cope, but at least I'm not numb, right?

So, after much thought and searching on how to incorporate some of Cassidy's ashes into a nice piece of jewelry of some kind, I finally found this beautiful memorial jewelry online and decided to order a ring with Cassidy's birthstone that could house a small amount of her ashes. It was a made-to-order ring, and it took forever to arrive. I was so happy when it finally got delivered. John helped me get the ashes in the ring and we screwed it all back together. I was finally able to keep a small piece of Cassidy (quite literally) with me at all times now. This was an emotional event, the first time getting up close and personal with her ashes like that. The mood was somber and solemn in a way. Almost reverent.

I soon noticed that the little screw that closes the ring wasn't quite tightening all the way. We tried everything: different-sized screwdrivers and Allen wrenches, with no luck. We went to a local jeweler to see if they could help. *No.* (Although the woman at the jeweler did recognize me from a local car commercial. So there's that). I went online to see if others who had ordered the same ring had similar issues, Nothing. Finally, I contacted the company that sold me the ring, and they had *never* had this issue before. What was so special about me? They agreed to send me out some additional screws of varying sizes to try and see if one worked. After weeks waiting on those, Nope! Nothing worked.

By this point, I was pissed. After trying every possible solution, the damn screw simply wouldn't tighten all the way. I was terrified that the screw would come out one day at just the wrong time and Cassidy's ashes would dump out in the toilet or sprinkle onto my scrambled eggs at breakfast.

As I sat amongst a plethora of tiny screws and even more tiny jewelry tools, I kind of lost it. I got so angry. I was becoming furious at Cassidy. This was so typical. Nothing was ever easy with her when she was alive and dammit, even in death she was making my life miserable. All I wanted was a nice way to remember my only child by carrying a pinch of her burnt body in a ring, and I couldn't even have that easily!

WTF, Cassidy?

I felt like she was out there somewhere in the universe orchestrating this whole mess and enjoying my stress and angst over it all. It wasn't fair! ... Then the tears came. Well, I felt like a hot mess at this point, and after the anger subsided a bit, I just felt plain silly for being so upset.

Once I got my bearings, I contacted the company once more, and they agreed to make a new ring and send it to me. A do-over. Much better. I knew there had to be a solution. This took another month. When the new ring finally arrived, it was like I could finally relax. We got all the things together to put the ashes into the new ring and send back the old defective one. Easy, right?

Guess again.

When I tried to get the screw out of the new ring to open the place where the ashes go, it wouldn't open. It was too *tight* for the Allen wrench to loosen it. I swear I'm not making this up. John tried it; we tried multiple tools. We did everything!

About this time, I just had to start laughing. Hysterically, actually. It was all so absurd. I just threw my hands up and surrendered. Okay, fine, you win, Cassidy. Is this your way of telling me you hate the ring? Well, message received, loud and clear.

So ... the brand new ring is, to this day, still sitting in its box, tucked inside of the funeral home insulated "lunch bag" that also houses Cassidy's cremains in a box. I'm not sure I will ever get her ashes in that ring to wear now. What seemed so important a few months ago seems frivolous now.

Now ... I just want to hug my daughter.

CHAPTER 16

GOING POSTAL

Today, I took care of something I had been putting off for a few weeks. I finally scooped a small amount of Cassidy's ashes to put into a little baggie inside of a tin. I placed it inside a mailer box, which went inside of a padded express mail envelope. On the padded mailer was a USPS label reading "cremated remains." This little Russian doll-like package was to be sent to a company called Artful Ashes in Seattle. They make beautiful hand-blown glass orbs with your loved one's ashes. I decided this would be a wonderful way to keep a tasteful memorial of Cassidy next to my bed without making my bedroom look like a funeral parlor. It was the perfect solution to the previous train wreck with the memorial ring.

The envelope was already pre-addressed by the glass company and ready to send via U.S. mail. Incidentally, when sending cremains, you must pay a special handling fee and use express mail requiring a signature. The cost was twenty-five dollars, if anyone is wondering.

I was proud of the way I handled getting her ashes in that container. I sat on the bed, next to John, and carefully opened the plastic bag that housed my portion of Cassidy (it never occurred to me before now, but wow, talk about splitting things evenly in a divorce). I didn't get overly emotional. Instead it felt reverent, respectful and peaceful. Everything was fine!

... well, perhaps I spoke too soon. The next day I went by myself to send it on its way. I pulled up to the post office ten minutes before closing. As I approached the door to enter, I said quietly to Cassidy and myself, "Looks look you're going on a little adventure."

Everything after that moment was horrible. The minute I stepped into the post office, I could feel the anxiety building. There was a long line, and as I stood waiting, clutching the package, if I'm being honest, I was hugging it. My breathing became labored, heavy: I felt tears welling up, and I tried not to fall apart in line. A huge lump formed in my throat, a giant rock on my chest; it was so hard to breathe. I clung to the parcel like I was protecting a valuable hidden treasure that people wanted to steal from me. It was *my* treasure.

All I could think of in that moment was the first time I sent Cassidy on an airplane by herself. She was ten, I think. She was so excited and so grown-up. And I was a wreck inside, but I held it together for her. I also flashed back to her first day of kindergarten. Her cute little backpack, an apple in one hand and a nap mat tucked under the other arm. She was so nervous, but she put her game face on and marched right into her class with a wave and an anxious smile. And I knew then just how hard that was for her; after all, Cassidy suffered from severe separation anxiety. At that moment in the post office, I felt exactly the same as I did in those moments from Cassidy's childhood. Those "firsts." I didn't want to let her go, but I knew it was go time. I had made it this far.

At last, it was my turn to go to the cashier/mail worker. Still trying not to cry. I put the package (once again, a portion of my daughter in a small box) onto the counter and said, "I need to send this," like it was the most normal thing to send at the post office. Just a normal day. Sending my daughter's burnt body via U.S. mail, like ya do ...

So, there's a big black label right on the padded envelope

that states "cremated remains." And yet the mail worker still proceeded to ask me, "Does this contain anything liquid, perishable, fragile, or potentially hazardous?" I am thinking to myself, well, theoretically, if one tried to snort the ashes, that could be hazardous. I don't think that's what he meant. Maybe it was the way I was staring at him blankly, but after a moment he said, "I'm sorry, I have to ask everyone." I managed to crack a tiny sad smile and then I proceeded to check the "no" box on the little computer screen. I paid my special handling fee, and then it was finished. Whew, I made it. Mission accomplished.

As I headed for the door ... All I could do was breathe, hard. A mantra that my yoga teacher says in class flashed into my brain, "If you don't want to change, don't breathe." I didn't want to feel like this forever, so all I could think to do was to breathe. What I didn't think about was that if you force yourself to breathe too rigorously, you will most likely exhale more than you inhale, and you may hyperventilate. Note to self: don't hyperventilate, it tends to make you feel anxious.

I finally made it to the door, still holding it together, somewhat—if you call a quivering lip holding it together. Until I made it outside. When the automatic door opened for me, I felt like I had burst through the finish line after a long race ... but then they tell you the first person through the ribbon actually loses. The tears continued to well up right behind my eyeballs. They were ready for the dam to break, almost overflowing by this point. Then, the minute I got inside my car and shut the door ... I fell apart. I mean ugly crying, tears falling like Niagara falls. *Why does this hurt so much?* Who knew that mailing your daughter to someone in Seattle, who will transform her ashes into a work of art, could hurt like this? If I had known, I would have asked John to do it.

The important thing to remember is everything is temporary, mostly feelings. And as I write this now, my feelings have already changed from that intensity I had a few hours ago. I am so excited to get the finished glass orb back in a few weeks. ... Another lesson I learned is never go to the post office alone again.

First day of Kindergarten, 1999

CHAPTER 17

MY MOM CARD HAS BEEN REVOKED

Tomorrow is Mother's Day. And it's not just any Mother's Day. Tomorrow will be the first Mother's Day for me that has a big fat question mark. Am I still a mother?

I know I would tell anyone else in the same situation that yes, of course you're still a mother. And yet it feels odd to celebrate Mother's Day now that my only child is gone. Like I'm undeserving. Like I lost my mother membership card. Like, "You couldn't keep your kid alive and safe? Sorry, you don't get to celebrate Mother's Day anymore." If Hallmark doesn't make a card about your situation, then it's probably not valid.

And to add insult to injury, my own mother died more than eleven years ago. Really, I've already had a new normal since then when it comes to celebrating this day. But until this year, I still remained a mother, myself, on active duty, and I felt entitled to be celebrated on Mother's Day. After all, I was a mother!

Back to the start ... here I am now, motherless and childless. What am I now? How do I define myself? When is my special day? Holidays have now been replaced by anniversaries.

Anniversaries of the day she died, the first Christmas without her, her first birthday since her death. All these firsts come with a soggy weight, like a big bag of rocks in my throat.

I remember when "firsts" were celebrated with applause, smiles and photographs. Cassidy's first steps, the first time she slept through the night, her first tooth, her first sleepover, her first day of school. Then there were those firsts that weren't so happy: her first fever, the first time she fell and skinned her knee, her first heartbreak, the first time she spent the night in a psych unit, her first stitches from self-inflicted cuts on her arms, the first time she shot heroin into her veins. (Yes, I went there. I have to.)

... Life wasn't always full of smiles, applause and photographs, you see. So here I am now, perhaps toughened up and better able to handle these new firsts in my own life, these "anniversaries" that will now mark time for me. My New Firsts are now full of tears, regret and old photographs.

So what will I do for Mother's Day? I'm honestly at a loss. I will most certainly shed some tears. Probably have constant flashbacks to better, happier times (thanks to Facebook). I might torture myself with regret. Ya know, while other mothers are enjoying mimosas, brunch, flowers and heartfelt, handwritten cards given by their children. There's a chance that after my pity party, I may try to enjoy a few happy moments with my newly acquired stepchildren (who aren't really children anymore) but are wonderful and loving to me nevertheless.

I know that whatever happens tomorrow, life will go on. I feel another chapter brewing inside me even now, which is a tad more inspirational and full of insight. But for today ... Not so much. Today, I am working on redefining motherhood for myself. Redefining my own identity, really, now that life has changed so drastically. I'll let you know what I come up with.

... *To be continued* ...

CHAPTER 18

MOTHERHOOD ... RE-IMAGINED

I am a mother. I grew a baby inside of my belly and birthed a child from my womb. I nourished her from my own breast and kept her safe and clean. I loved her unconditionally. I raised her and cared for her until she was an adult and left home. Even then, I continued to worry about her every day, praying that she was safe and happy. I know that many times she wasn't. I never stopped loving her. She didn't make it past age twenty-two. And I still remain her mother.

But motherhood isn't a title earned by the act of childbirth or breastfeeding. One earns the title of mother by the love she gives. The care and feeding, the nurturing and kindness she exhibits to her "children." And make no mistake, when I say "children," I speak of the ones who live in her home and call her Mom, yes ... and I also speak of the ones who she teaches after school or takes care of until bedtime. I speak of the ones who she befriends and mentors. Those who she for some reason takes an interest in and inspires to be successful through her example, advice or friendship. A mother earns the title by showing up, by being present and being available.

I was fortunate enough not only to have been a mother to Cassidy, my biological child, but also a mother figure and nurturer to countless children and young people through my work, my life, my teaching and directing over my lifetime so far. A year ago, I legally became a stepmother to John's wonderful, loving children. Since losing Cassidy, it has become abundantly clear to me that I still have a multitude of reasons to proudly call myself a MOM. I claim that title with honor now.

I woke today to a barrage of messages and thoughtful Facebook posts wishing me Happy Mother's Day. Friends and family who knew today would be a struggle. My first Mother's Day without my only child. Then, while drinking my coffee in the kitchen, my twenty-two-year-old stepdaughter, Rachel, brought me the sweetest bouquet of flowers. Later, we all went to brunch, my husband and his three children who live with us now (ages twenty-two, twenty and seventeen).

After a couple mimosas, they gave me the sweetest gift bag with a card. The card is what got me. All three wrote a personal note inside that cut right through to my tender heart and brought me to tears right there at the restaurant. Tears flowed as I thanked them all for making my Mother's Day so special. I admitted to them that Mother's Days weren't always like this. When you have a child that suffers from SUD, holidays tended to get chaotic, and they weren't always the way you dreamed they would be. I was so grateful this afternoon for that "normal" Mother's Day moment. There I was, enjoying a normal brunch with this well-adjusted family that I am now a part of. No drama, no chaos.

There was a photo posted on a Child Loss Support Facebook group recently, of a beautiful sunset with these words: "If you were here, everything would be okay."

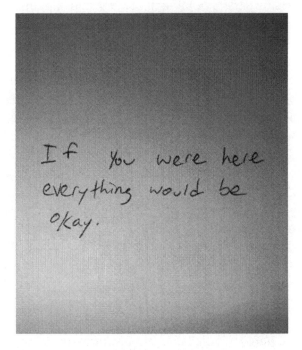

Bullshit! No it wouldn't.

The reality would not line up with this fantasy. I get it. We want to lift up our deceased children to some unattainable mythology. But the reality is, I mourn the potential, the possible future of Cassidy. Not the actual Cassidy. My relationship with her when she died was fractured, broken. We had been geographically separated for awhile, and I had finally started to find serenity in my life as I worked on accepting the things out of my control. We had recently started the long process of reconnecting in a meaningful way, and it was still a struggle and a constant question mark as to her sobriety and health. What I miss isn't the Cassidy who was in active addiction. I mourn for what might have been. For those imagined future moments with her when everything is okay and we are doing the mother-daughter things that I always dreamed of. Planning a wedding, helping her pick out furniture for her first home. Buying her maternity clothes and decorating a nursery. Holding her hand as she gives birth, and holding my first grand baby in my arms as I cry tears of love and gratitude. But if I'm being completely honest, all that was not really in the cards for Cassidy. That really was just a fantasy.

So here I am living in my reality. My present moment. It looks a lot different now. Acceptance is the key. Accepting that *that* future cannot happen now. Accepting a different reality. Life without Cassidy ... *Sigh*. It hurts even typing it.

This I know: my present moment doesn't discount any past experiences. In fact, my present moment is what it is because of my past. I am who I am because of any pain, sorrow, loss, joy, excitement, hardships, and successes that I have gone through up till now.

I am a mother. I will always be a mother. I claim that with pride, humility, gratitude and love. Cassidy made me a mother almost twenty-three years ago. I will be a mother till my last breath.

Happy Mother's Day to anyone out there who identifies as a mother. Claim the title if you feel entitled to it. Redefine it, reclaim it. It's yours.

CHAPTER 19

CASSIDY'S ALUMNI VISIT ... IN A PLASTIC BAG

I had the opportunity recently to visit and speak with the girls currently in treatment at Sunrise, the therapeutic boarding school/residential treatment center in Southern Utah where Cassidy spent eight months of her adolescence, after we learned the full extent of her drug and psychiatric issues. I had been shooting a film all week in St. George, and on my final day in the area, I arranged to go speak at Sunrise. When I contacted them to offer myself, I had no idea what I wanted to say. I simply felt compelled to go. So I followed my instincts and did it. It was the best decision I could have made.

Up until two days before I was to speak, I still had no idea how to organize my thoughts or what these girls needed to hear from a mother who lost her daughter to the same thing they are currently struggling with. After all, we had lost our battle, and they and their families were still at war. I knew exactly how I wanted to start my speech, and I had the forethought to bring along the necessary props, but I was getting stuck in the details.

I had the morning off from filming and took the opportunity to drive to a spot where we had gone with Cassidy on a family weekend while she was in treatment. It was near the Quail Creek Reservoir. My plan was to spread a small portion of her ashes there. After hiking a bit, I found the perfect quiet spot near some wildflowers and red rocks. I opened the small baggie and gave Cassidy back to nature, back to this spot where she had stood in her mortal covering years before. A time when she had hope! Tears streamed down my face at this ritual. Then as I turned to walk back down the trail, a single white butterfly flitted in front of me. It took my breath away. I felt her; I knew Cassidy was here. I followed the butterfly for a bit, then she followed me, and eventually she turned and disappeared in the direction of the spot where I had left her ashes. My tears of sadness had turned into tears of joy. My face was beaming, not just a smile, but pure joy filled me. It was just the message I needed from her. I drove away that morning with a new calm purpose. I felt so loved, so grateful.

As I continued to struggle with what I would say, John was kind enough to write me a first draft after talking with me on the phone about a rough idea of what was on my mind and in my heart. He knew me well enough to know where to start, and so he did. I couldn't have done it without him. Once I had a draft, it was easy to fill in the blanks, and my message became clear. But what surprised me is that until I got in front of those girls, I had no idea how I would finish, and what I ended up saying to them in the end was exactly what they needed to hear *and* what I needed to say. In fact, it was what Cassidy needed to say to them and to me. That message was *Love!*

On Thursday, May 25, 2017, I arrived at Sunrise, in Hurricane, Utah, a small town just outside of St. George and at the edge of Zion National Park. Red rock country! As I pulled up to the house, I could feel my insides doing backflips. After all, the last time I was here was for Cassidy's graduation from the program six years ago, in May 2011.

As I sat in my car, every memory of this place, good and bad, came flooding back. I remembered the first day we brought her here. When she found out she would have to take her piercings out after the tour, she ran to the car and wouldn't go back in. I remember bargaining with her and the therapists saying, "It's 100 degrees out there, she will eventually come back in." They were right. I remember crying in that same parking spot seven years ago after we left our sixteen-year-old daughter there with strangers and no contact for three weeks. It was the worst kind of separation anxiety. I also remember pulling into this space when Chris and I arrived to spend our first therapeutic family weekend with Cassidy. I was so excited to wrap my arms around her and reassure her that everything was okay, that we loved her!

So there I sat, about to walk through those doors again. This time, there would be no Cassidy waiting on the other side, ready for a hug. This time, I carried Cassidy inside a small box that housed a heavy-duty plastic bag filled with her ashes, the only physical part of her that remains.

I was just as anxious and agitated as I thought I would be once I went inside. But I was also calmed just being there. The house was heavy with memories and familiar energy. As they set me up in the great room, I was brought back to the last time I was in that room. Cassidy's graduation. A day filled with hope for a bright future. Cassidy's beautiful, happy smile, her bright eyes that poured with tears of joy for all she had accomplished and sadness for all the friends she would leave behind to continue on their journey. And also the fear for what awaited her outside of this safe haven, this cocoon.

As the girls started to gather on the gigantic sectional and the comfortable floor, I was preparing by getting a smiling image of Cassidy up on the large screen at the front of the room. I was ready. As the clinical director introduced me, I stepped in front of the group of about forty teenage girls looking up at me, Cassidy's beautiful image behind me ... and then tears, a flood of emotions as I started to speak. Once I gathered myself and wiped the tears away temporarily, I began. I pulled out the clear plastic bag that housed Cassidy ashes and as I introduced myself to the girls, "Hi, I'm Charla, and *this* is my daughter

Cassidy," I plopped the bag of ashes onto the stool next to me. "On November 11, 2016, she died of a drug overdose. She was twenty-two."

... the room fell suddenly silent and I could feel the energy shift, followed swiftly by the sound of sniffles, gasps. I could sense the fear, sadness, angst. This was how I introduced my daughter. What followed was possibly the most impactful hour of my life thus far.

CHAPTER 20

THE SPEECH

After introducing myself and Cassidy to the girls, I continued my speech ...

Six years ago, Cassidy was right where you are today, quite literally. In fact, she was in this very room. She may have even slept in one of the beds you will go to sleep in tonight. Cassidy, like you, had her whole life ahead of her. Cassidy, like some of you, thought she was invincible. She thought that even though death was a possibility with the high-risk behaviors she engaged in, she didn't believe it was a probability. But she was wrong. She was dead wrong.

My daughter Cassidy Aspen Cochran suffered from Anxiety, Depression, a personality disorder, and Substance Use Disorder, a disease that, when left untreated, can be fatal. In Cassidy's case, it was. Her father and I found out that she was shooting up heroin after her then-boyfriend overdosed in our home in her bedroom. She was fifteen years old. Some would say she was just a child. After all, we did find her needles hiding in her childhood teddy bear. But she wasn't just "a child"; she was our child, our only child. My daughter, for whom her father and I would have walked to the ends of the earth to protect or done anything to help end the self-destructive behaviors that ultimately destroyed her.

My daughter is now in here, ashes in this bag next to me. I am sure this is not the Sunrise alumni visit Cassidy had in mind after she walked out through the front doors after eight months of treatment, a Sunrise graduate. Because Cassidy was hopeful about her future six years ago. So was everyone who loved her.

Initially, Cassidy resisted us, and the idea of extended treatment. She used all the negative tools of manipulation, lying, and tantrum-throwing to avoid coming here. We even had to give her a sedative that her doctor prescribed, just to get her on the airplane. In her first month at Sunrise, she would write letters to us saying she was being abused here as well as mistreated, starved and neglected. There were no depths to which she wouldn't sink, to try and avoid facing the truth about her life. After all, she was young, and things didn't seem real. Death didn't seem real. Threatening suicide was her ultimate manipulation she would use to try to hurt me and her father, and to get her way.

Now, we realize it wasn't Cassidy's desire to hurt us but it was her disease, heroin's grip on her mind and body, that told her to do whatever it took to get it more heroin. No matter who it hurt emotionally, financially, or physically, heroin was determined to feed itself through her veins. In reality, the person who it hurt the most was Cassidy. After a couple months of fighting things here at Sunrise, she finally had her epiphany. She made the decision to start to help herself.

My daughter was like a light switch. Either all off, or all on. Once she made that decision, she not only chose treatment, she decided she was going to take all her new friends with her. Cassidy always had a heart of gold. Once her eyes opened to a better life, she was determined to help everyone else around her get well, too. That is who she was. A natural leader, she started to rally her new friends to join her in defeating this disease that had gotten a hold of her and refused to let go. She started to journal quite a bit and to write us at home. She apologized for all she had put us through. She knew we loved her unconditionally. She started to understand the consequences of her actions. Cassidy started to heal.

I allowed myself for the first time in a long time to be hopeful for our future as a family and finally having my little girl back. All the dreams a mom has for her daughter. Sending Cassidy off to college. Helping her pick out her wedding dress and make plans for her wedding. Picking out things to furnish her new apartment. And finally holding her hand as I see my first grand baby being born. Holding my baby's baby. Singing to her or him as I did to their mother when she was a baby in my arms. I was hopeful again that she would continue using the skills that would help her stay clean.

After she left Sunrise, we were so proud that she had decided to live a life that was full of joy and love rather than anguish and sorrow. But then it happened: about two months after she had come home for good, she disappeared for a night, found her old boyfriend, and she used once again. It was that easy.

We understand that sobriety is a lifelong commitment and people have relapses. It happens. But instead of getting up, dusting herself off, and moving forward again with skills she knew, she sank right back into the quicksand. I don't know if it was peer pressure or her answering the siren's song of her old nemesis, heroin, who promised her heaven, but only gave her hell. Cassidy followed heroin back into the sea of self-destruction.

We danced the dance all over again. The lies, the deception. Her disappearing and reappearing. Jumping from one using boyfriend to the next. Weeks became months, and months became years. She had brushes with death multiple times. She stopped breathing, and CPR had to be performed to bring her back. She kept using. She contracted hepatitis C from a dirty needle. She kept using. She overdosed one time so severely that she lost her hearing. She was deaf for two weeks before her hearing slowly came back. She kept using. She spent time in jail, she spent time in hospitals. She started using meth and cut her arms wide open one day in a fit of rage. She had multiple close friends die of overdoses. She would clean up for a bit, then time would pass and the siren would sing her song again, calling Cassidy to follow.

After a short stay in jail, she decided to use with a cell mate who made a few calls to have her "friends" pick her up when she was released. Cassidy ended up in a real-life *Breaking Bad* situation. A meth lab and heroin den complete with someone duct-taped to a pole who barely looked alive. She called her father in a panic to come pick her up.

He didn't know if he was being led to an ambush, to be killed so they could steal his money and car. Her father, who would go to the ends of the earth for his little girl, now was trying to figure out if she was luring him to his death. He finally had the good sense to have Cassidy use her powers of manipulation to get a ride to the Waffle House, where he felt safe to pick her up in public. When he got her in the car, he said "I'm sorry, I cannot allow you back into my home unless you are clean."

He, dying on the inside and crying on the outside, drove his only child to a homeless shelter for women in downtown Birmingham. Then he said, through a cracking voice and streams of tears running down his face, "If you don't stop using and turn things around, you will be dead within the year." It was painfully prophetic. A prophecy you don't ever want to think, much less say out loud. Time in a homeless shelter turned things around … for a moment.

She promised to get clean and get back into appropriate treatment, looking for a long-term solution to tackle her disease. And yet another boyfriend. She seemed to be doing better. We believed she had been clean for a few months by now. She seemed to have a purpose again, even if it was taking care of the new boyfriend. They got bored one night after he got paid and decided to use together. He picked up what he thought was heroin, but it turned out to be straight fentanyl. They both shot up. Her boyfriend stood up and fell into the bathtub. Cassidy slumped over and breathed her last. She was found when her boyfriend awoke, on her knees with her head on the ground, in a position known in yoga as "Child's Pose."

Cassidy was twenty-two years old. Cassidy sat right where you are sitting, six years ago. She slept in a bed in a room upstairs here at Sunrise six years ago. Cassidy's cremains sit next to me right here, right now. That is my new "normal."

Not a day goes by that I don't ache for my daughter. I mourn what could have been as well as what was. As a parent you are given the task first and foremost to protect your child, as your parents have obviously done by sending you here. As we did for Cassidy. I know some of you are angry with them for sending you here. Some of you are still furious and shut down.

But your parents can only do so much. It is *you* that must decide to live. It is *you* that must decide to heal. It is *you* that must decide whatever happens in life, that you will choose sobriety. If you don't, you will not only destroy your own lives, but the lives of every person who loves you.

(I then showed the last few minutes of the memorial video we showed at Cassidy's celebration of life. I wanted to show them that Cassidy was more than her illness. She was just like them.)

Life can be unpredictable, and life sure as hell will be painful at times. I stand here with my daughter in a bag! Nobody deserves to go through that. Nobody. Don't make the ones who love you suffer more than they already have. Don't *you* suffer any more than you already have. Don't come back to Sunrise in a bag inside a little black box like Cassidy did. Come back and declare to those who are lost, that there is a better way. That there is hope! You have to make the choice every single day for the rest of your lives to live that better way.

There is no guarantee that life will be easy. In fact, pain is inevitable, it's suffering that's optional. The key is acceptance! I also believe the key lies in connection to others. Reaching out for help, being vulnerable, accepting help and helping yourself. You can do this. There are a lot of people out there who love you. And I believe that each one of you has at least one other person who loves you with unfailing and unconditional love. And *you*, as much as anyone else in the entire universe, deserve that love and affection. Accept it. It's yours. Then the real magic happens when you start to love yourself. When you start to forgive yourself. I received a message from Cassidy after she died. She said, "It's okay to be okay now. We've all suffered enough. The time to heal is now, and this now has never existed before … don't worry, love saves everyone in the end. That love is inside you and surrounding you now. It's where I live now, inside you. Love lives in you."

This is what Cassidy needed me to tell you today. It's all about *Love*. With love, comes healing. I believe in you!

CHAPTER 21

CASSIDY'S ALUMNI VISIT, PART 2

So there I stood, shaken and weepy, sharing my innermost thoughts about grief and loss with a large group of teenage girls in a residential treatment program, far removed from friends and family. As I told my story, I was acutely aware of the expressions on the girls' faces looking up at me that afternoon. Tear-streaked cheeks, stone-faced stares, angry jaws, compassionate eyes—you name it. Each one of those girls was hearing an entirely different speech coming from my lips, based on where they were at that moment. And when I finished and opened it up for questions and comments, that's when the real magic happened. Something I didn't expect.

Several girls commented that never before could they conceive of the way their behavior had affected their parents. They suddenly felt empathy for what their parents have been going through all this time. One girl said through tears streaming down her face, "When you talked about your daughter threatening suicide and manipulating you, I saw myself in that, and I never realized how it affected my mom. I am so sorry for what you have been through, and I'm so sorry for the way I've treated my parents."

Another girl told me she was graduating tomorrow from

the program after a year. She was terrified that her story would end like Cassidy's story did. She confided in me that this was the motivation she needed to stay clean. She said, "I won't come back here the way your daughter did. I can't."

More girls shared their stories and the struggles they have had with their parents. So many others offered their heartfelt condolences to me for the loss of my daughter, who I know in my heart they identified with. The overriding theme of the day was the regret they felt for the way they had treated their parents in the throes of their addiction. It was clear they didn't want to treat them that way. What I saw behind those painful young eyes was remorse, empathy, and suffering. It broke my heart. This was a room full of young women; hell, girls, really. They were all in pain, most hating themselves for one reason or another. Alienated from family and friends. Shut off from the world due to some distant choice they made that changed everything for them!

What I saw was a group of girls, grasping for connection; lost, in desperate need of love. Most importantly, they needed to love themselves. I told them over and over that they were loved and they deserved their own love and affection. That is the message that Cassidy wanted to get through to them. I am sure of that now. I hope they heard me, I hope they heard Cassidy. In the end, I could only do so much, and I knew it wasn't my job to save them. My job was to tell my story, to tell Cassidy's story. She would have done the same thing if she were alive today.

This is how I will honor Cassidy now. It's all suddenly clear. Even though she is snuffed out physically, she will *not* be silenced. I will see to that. Her story is one of suffering, regret, chaos, and *Love*. The most important thing being love. This is how I can honor her, and I will do it willingly, with a full heart and tears in my red eyes.

... Just love each other, and love yourself. How hard is that? This is where healing starts. If only I had been able to get that message through to Cassidy before it was too late. But perhaps this is what Cassidy is trying to get through to me now. Message received, loud and clear.

CHAPTER 22

BORN TO ME ... CASSIDY

Twenty-three years ago today, my sweet baby gulped her first breath of air. She had been growing inside my body for nine months, in a liquid-filled, crowded cocoon: safe, protected, nurtured. But twenty-three years ago on this very day, she was ready for a change of environment, she was ready to emerge from that only world she had known inside of me and take on a brand-new world. She didn't know what she was getting herself into. Neither did we.

Those first few moments after her birth were full of emotions, slime, tears, euphoria, tiny newborn baby cries and ignorance. We knew nothing back then, and it turns out that seven months ago when Cassidy breathed her last breath, we still knew nothing.

Today we celebrate Cassidy's birthday. That sounds strange. She is not gaining a year this time. It is merely a symbolic celebration, a marker of what would have been, what could have been. She will forever be twenty-two now. That was the last birthday she celebrated, and there will be no more. I'm sure Cassidy would have loved the repeating numbers surrounding her death. She was one of those people who always connected with 11:11. Every time she noticed that time on a clock, she would stop what she was doing, close her eyes and make a wish, then kiss her fingers and blow it into the air. It was her ritual. She was twenty-two when she died, her birthday on the twenty-second. She died on November 11 (11/11), eleven years (to the week) after her grandma died. (A side note: I just realized as I went to publish it that this is chapter twenty-two. Ha, nice work, Universe.)

Now, since Cassidy's death, I see 11:11 everywhere. It has become a little wink and nod from Cassidy. It always makes me smile.

As I write this chapter, I am trying to figure out exactly what it is I want to say. I find myself at a loss for words. So I will keep it brief. Today is the anniversary of the day Cassidy was born to me, to her father. I have decided to reclaim June 22. It belongs to us now. Those left behind. Twenty-three years ago, it was my day just as much as it was hers. It was my first day to meet my baby girl outside of myself. It was the beginning of a beautiful relationship, and a hard one, if I'm being honest. I will forever celebrate the day of Cassidy's birth in a new way. With cake, or without, no presents, maybe a pedicure, a toast to unrealized moments that will never become memories. A new type of celebration of the day everything changed. Love was born to me. After all, Cassidy reminded me how to truly love, like getting a love booster shot. I initially learned it from my mother. Now those two are reunited and hopefully celebrating in their own non-mortal way, today and always.

Until someone dies, their birthday marks their beginning. The start to an unknown end (as we know we won't live forever). The hard part now is that her beginning, her birthday, has another new meaning. A beautiful start to a tragic end, which has now been marked, recorded. Bookends, now noted in her obituary.

Happy Birthday, my Cassidy!

CHAPTER 23

WE ACCEPT THE LOVE WE THINK WE DESERVE

Warning: this chapter is not pretty. It's ugly and it's painful!

I will never forget rushing into the ER at Northridge Hospital one evening after getting a call that Cassidy had been taken there by ambulance. I walked in to witness the damage she had done to herself that night. Arms cut wide open, bleeding. She hit an artery this time.

Her then-boyfriend had found her in the bathroom, blood everywhere. Cassidy had been a "cutter" for most of her adolescence. It was something she had been in treatment for and worked on since she was twelve. But this time was different. This was a real attempt to end it. I knew it. I had never seen it this bad, despite all the trips to urgent care for stitches in the past. What I found out later is that Cassidy and this boyfriend had been using together for quite awhile ... meth this time. He was just another toxic relationship in her long history of "bad" boyfriends. The meth made her so agitated, paranoid, and anxious that anything would set her off, and being around her at that time was like being with a ticking time bomb that was set to go off randomly, over and over.

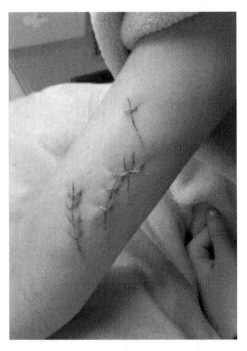

Sometimes she would go off and hurt herself physically, or hurt those around her emotionally. Other times, she would be the one on the other side of a "man" she thought she loved exploding and hurting her physically and emotionally. This was one of those times in Cassidy's life that still haunts me. I have to keep reminding myself that these instances were all part of Substance Use Disorder. Her disease and the other underlying psychiatric disorders she suffered (anxiety, depression, possible personality disorders) all worked together like an orchestrated mess to make her feel worthless, unloved, angry, and hopeless. This was the canvas on which every bad relationship could spill and splat its horrendous muddy colors, covering her with blood, bruises, track marks, scars and self-hatred.

Every one of these incidents came with a boatload of lies. Some sketchy explanation that didn't add up. Until eventually the truth peered out and we could see the real story. "He got jealous because he found an old flirty text to another guy." "He accused me of cheating on him." "He got messed up at a party and lost his shit on me."

... Some truths we never quite got to. Those stories sit on me like a million pounds. I will never know what really happened the night she told us that she was assaulted in Southside last October. Her dad and I suspected right away that her boyfriend had gone off on her for some unknown reason. This was the damage that night:

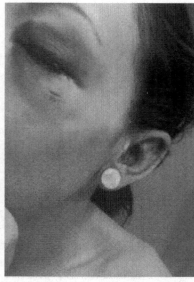

She died less than a month after this happened. It still turns my stomach to see her bruised and beaten this way. And the sentiment that keeps running through my head brings me to tears again: "We accept the love we think we deserve."

The fact that she hated herself enough to accept boyfriends who would do this to her is the greatest travesty of all. It hurts me to know she was hurt this way by men who told her they loved her. It's easy to sit in our pretty homes, in our comfortable chairs, on our fancy laptops or iPhones, far removed from anything icky or uncomfortable. But this is what's happening to people you know. Your own daughters, sons, friends, neighbors.

This is what Substance Use Disorder can look like. *This* is what mental illness looks like, which leads to self-medication that can lead to addiction. It's horrific. It's ugly, it hurts. And we're not even the ones suffering. Imagine how it feels for those who are. I'm still trying to figure out what happened to my only daughter during her short life. I'm striving to understand what life was really like for her. I want to see it from her perspective. It's only through understanding and empathy that we can truly change things.

I'm afraid I judged Cassidy wrongly at times when she was at her lowest. I was the one who was charged with loving her unconditionally all her life, and if I'm being honest, there were moments in her life when she was hard to love. However, I always tried to understand her, and I think I will spend the rest of my own life continuing to do just that.

That's why I am writing the book. It's my therapy, I suppose. My way of dusting off the skeletons in my own closet. Regret is a horrible feeling. So I won't live in a vat of regret; instead, I will try to bathe in a sea of acceptance and true understanding. My daughter suffered very much. It wasn't my fault *and* I could have done a lot better.

CHAPTER 24

LIVING WITHOUT HER ... RANDOM THOUGHTS WHILE GRIEVING

Life is hard. Harder than it used to be, only ... not. As Cassidy's dad says: "The presence of her absence is everywhere." ... And it is so very thick. It physically hurts at times. No one can imagine this pain until it happens to them, and I wouldn't wish it on anyone.

Sometimes I can't catch my breath. It feels like someone punched me in the stomach unexpectedly. Like getting the wind knocked out of you. In those moments, I want to disappear. Nothing matters but my pain and wanting it gone now. I want her back *now*.

Or rather, I want the fantasy back of how things could be. Perhaps what I crave is to live in a parallel universe where Cassidy and I have the healthiest relationship ever, and she is clean and thriving and reaching her full, amazing potential. Finding someone to love her and then that someone treating her the way she always deserved. Giving me a grandchild eventually. Spending holidays together. Wonderful stuff. But that's impossible now.

Now, I have a new normal. *Now*, all I have are photographs and memories of a past that sometimes sucked, and other times it was the best life ever! Full of smiles, laughter and fun together. Movies, music, crafts, fondue, theme parks, beaches, Broadway shows, road trips, family dinners, adventures in the rain, ski trips and hot chocolate. We had a wonderful life together ... sometimes ... (record skip) ... when Cassidy wasn't self-destructing.

My New Normal now is that I burst into tears at the most unexpected moments, and then I'm perfectly fine. In the car, the bathroom, walking through the grocery store, looking for my car in a parking lot, getting a pedicure, riding an elevator, wherever. I don't understand how grief can induce anxiety like that. I didn't experience this with the loss of my mother. But with Cassidy, this unnatural loss, it's like taking meth (or at least that's how I imagine it would feel) jittery, on edge and panicked. Nothing feels quite normal or right. My regular calm has been obliterated, and it only occasionally rears its wonderful head into my otherwise crazy new world.

One night, I had a panic attack trying to fall asleep. All I could see running through my mind as I closed my eyes was Cassidy's body burning in the crematorium. Over and over, the image of her body in flames—an image I never witnessed in real life, only imagined in its most horrific details. It's a horrible image and one I couldn't shake. I felt my breath quicken, my heart race; a lump formed in my belly, my chest. The tears flowed—angry, panicked tears. I asked John to hold me until the feeling subsided (well, that and a half of a Xanax helped). Finally, all was okay for a moment. Peace, long enough to drift off.

Hours later, I would wake to memories of her cold dead body. Touching her shoulder covered by the white cotton sheet at the funeral home. Her ice-cold cheek and forehead against my warm lips. The feeling of her soft hair under my fingers. The memory is so visceral it hurts, and yet I hope I never, ever forget how it all felt!

There are other random feelings, thoughts that plague me

now. Like, the fact that my genetic legacy is finished with Cassidy's death. My DNA has reached the end of the line. It's a sad and existential awareness. Not only has the door to my physical legacy slammed shut with my only child's death, but also, the only person who knew me the way she did is gone. Forever! She understood me, like only a daughter could. She got that I was obsessed with making beds, and she knew what I liked to add to mac and cheese to make it amazing. Only Cassidy appreciated the ridiculous cheese fondue recipe of my mother's that called for Velveeta, *and* she loved that fricking fondue with a passion. Only Cassidy got that I secretly liked to binge-watch reality TV shows like *Untold Stories of the ER* and *Dance Moms*. She got that I still cried when I heard the song, "I Hope You Dance," and shared the memory with me of spoiling my mom in NYC after we found out she had less than a year to live. So many shared experiences and shared traumas. I felt as if Cassidy and I were like war buddies in a way, after all we had been through together.

Then another quandary enters my mind: Who gets my stuff now when I die? Who would even want it? Which begs the question: why do I keep anything of sentimental value now at all? My mother's wedding dress, my own wedding dress, family photos, Cassidy's baby book, a quilt my mother made ... you get the picture.

It makes me rethink everything I thought I knew. The natural order of things hasn't happened. She died first. My newly acquired stepchildren are all practically grown, and they have no attachment to any of the sentimental items from my life. So, what now? When I die, no one will have any attachment to those tangible things. They will most likely gather all my stuff into boxes and tote it down to Goodwill. They won't remember why I kept the little heart-shaped sterling silver charm on my dresser, or why I have an old hankie of my mom's in a jewelry box, or the story of my childhood boyfriend who gave me the gold identity bracelet when I moved away at age eleven. No one will have any desire to go through all the home videos or family photos from my earlier lifetime. After all, it's just *stuff,* and stuff without the memories looks a lot like junk.

And yet, *stuff* has become so important to me since Cassidy died. I woke from a dream a few months ago obsessing about her pink blanket. It was a baby quilt I made all by myself when I was about twelve years old, as a 4-H project. It won a blue ribbon at the fair. I was so proud of that quilt and decided then and there that I would keep it and wrap my future baby in it one day. Well, I did fourteen years later, and that pink blanket became one of Cassidy's treasures. Even into her preteen years, she could be seen with it wrapped around her shoulders watching TV. When I woke that particular morning, I panicked because I had no idea where that blanket was. To this day, I still don't know where it ended up, and it rips me apart. I want it! I want to hold it and smell it and feel its tattered edges.

I get it ... it ain't nothing but a thing. But it was *her* thing.

I now carry Cassidy's driver's license in my wallet. I'm not sure why. They write the date of death on it with a Sharpie, so you can't steal the deceased person's identity. It was in the bag of her personal belongings collected by the coroner. It was the only item I wanted to keep from that bag. After all, I didn't have much use for nipple rings or cigarettes.

CHAPTER 25

WAITING …FOR A MIRACLE

I haven't felt like writing lately. In fact, if I'm being honest with myself, I haven't *felt* much of anything lately. Just another stop in one of those pesky stages of grief, I suppose.

So here I sit … Watching time trickle by without her. Sometimes I'm sentimental about all things Cassidy, but lately I find myself stuck somewhere between angry and numb. I am startled by my reactions or lack thereof, when I see a photo of her shared on Facebook lately. It cuts like a knife for a moment, then my defenses start construction on a nice sturdy fence to protect my vulnerable heart. I suppose it's all part of the journey, as they say. I would rather change my itinerary or get a full refund for canceling the trip, thank you very much. But alas, that wasn't part of the contract, so I will stay on this train until it gets where it's going. I'll be enjoying the scenery along the way, perhaps getting motion sickness around the sharp curves and undoubtedly missing what I couldn't bring with me this time.

Damnit, I miss her. It's as simple as that.

I remember getting so homesick when I went off to Connecticut right after high school to be a nanny. I was so homesick that it made me physically ill. I cried so hard that I actually started to hyperventilate. Those few weeks felt like torture until I was able to quit the job and come back home. That's how it feels missing Cassidy sometimes. And yet I know full well there is no "quitting" or "coming home" this time.

This is my biggest lesson in acceptance right here. It's the most challenging lesson I've encountered so far in my life. Some days I pass the acceptance test with flying colors and high honors ... And yet today, I just want to change the past.

CHAPTER 26

THE QUEEN OF MAKE-BELIEVE

I am the Queen of Make-believe! Actually, it sounded more like this: "I am the Queen of Make-a-Beeve!" That's what our precocious little two-year-old Cassidy loudly and proudly proclaimed herself to be (with a crown on her soft blond hair, undoubtedly). And boy howdy, was she ever. Always dreaming up some fantasy or imaginary scenario for herself and those around her. She had more dress-up clothes than regular clothes. Cassidy wouldn't have been Cassidy without a tiara, fairy wings or a wand of some kind. When she was probably two, there was a solid month during which she insisted on being called Roo (from Winnie the Pooh). She and I went to visit my family in Utah during that time, and Cassidy continued her fantasy there, adding that her grandmother would be dubbed Kanga while we were in town. Every time someone called her Cassidy on that visit, she politely and with great frustration underneath, corrected them in her two-year-old way, struggling with the "r" as usual: "I'm Woo." She could keep up this game of make-believe for weeks, never dropping character.

When she was in third grade, we got a note sent home from her teacher one day, concerned over the fact that Cassidy refused to write her own name on worksheets and classwork, etc.

Apparently, she would write, *Mipsy Aspen Old Navy* or *Candy* instead of her given name. This bothered her teacher enough to ask for our support from home. But her dad and I both didn't really care, nor could we understand why it mattered all that much. I mean, what's so wrong with the healthy imagination of an eight-year-old? Am I right?

I realized recently that, since her death, I have taken the throne. It's not suppose to work that way, I know, but when your daughter dies at the age of twenty-two, nothing really ever is as it should be, nor will it ever be again. So here I now sit on the Glitter Throne. I have rightly now become the Queen of Make-believe, a title handed down to me by my beautiful daughter. I mean really, here I am pretending like everything is perfectly fine, after finding out nine months ago that my daughter died on her bathroom floor, of a drug overdose.

Perhaps she inherited that imagination from me. I'm an actor. I've made a career out of creating believability on screen or on stage, living under imaginary circumstances. And my life after losing Cassidy has been no exception. I can pretend my way through anything. When my real life circumstances are too painful, I can easily slide into another set of imaginary circumstances to make life more bearable.

I fantasize that she is in "a better place." That she's in a physical place called heaven or something like that. In my fantasy, it's like summer camp. No responsibilities, just lazy afternoons at the lake, with activities like archery, swimming, painting and horseback riding. At dusk, a campfire with s'mores and hot chocolate ...

(Record skip) ...

Okay, wait—Cassidy didn't love summer camp. Those couple weeks in the summer were usually filled with anxiety, tears and desperate letters home, pleading with us to pick her up and get her out of there.

She went to Camp Cosby, which happens to be on the same lake where her mama bear and papa bear live (that is what we called her paternal grandparents). One day during camp, they decided to go for a boat ride down by Camp Cosby to see if they could catch a glimpse of nine-year-old Cassidy. Well, they did, and what they saw was Cassidy waving excitedly on the shore while involved in water sports, and they reported back that she looked like she was having the best time. Come to find out later, the truth was that when she saw their boat, she started jumping up and down to get their attention, waving her arms wildly and yelling (which they couldn't hear), "GET ME OUT OF HERE! THANK GOD YOU'VE COME TO RESCUE ME!"

Well, you can imagine her disappointment when they continued past with smiles on their faces and innocent waves goodbye.

So I take it back: heaven is not like summer camp.

How about this? In my fantasy, Cassidy, her grandma and her uncle Boo are all spending the rest of eternity, or whatever you believe, at the most amazing yoga retreat ever. Calm and peaceful. I'll throw in a harp for good measure. But mostly there is chanting and people meditating. Bare feet, big smiles, and happy hearts. And chocolate, lots of chocolate. Also a giant screen TV where the heaven residents can choose to watch any loved one still on Earth, and send secret messages of their choosing. (A butterfly, a bird, a whisper, you name it.) In this land of make-believe heaven, there is music and art and softness, rooms filled with cloud pillows, white sand beaches and most importantly love. An abundance of LOVE.

Ok, so realistically, I know I have no earthly idea what happens when one dies. But I seriously think I would wither away in my grief if I didn't have that fantasy of what the afterlife is like for Cassidy. I have to believe that she is enjoying herself in her most perfect form, free from anxiety, depression, cravings, and self-loathing. I must believe that she is free, happy, and filled with the most pure love in the universe.

I know that during her life, she created her own imaginary circumstances just to cope. She used a variety of tools/weapons. From playing dress-up as a toddler, to pretending she was Roo for a week at grandma's, to getting involved in theatre as a child, to getting lost in Harry Potter books and movies. All the way to eventually sticking a needle in her arm to go someplace else for a while. A seemingly better place than she was before.

Little did she know that it was a lie. There's a slippery slope between engaging in a healthy game of make-believe and attempting to escape a reality from which you can never come back.

Now, Cassidy can never come back to me. And that is something that no amount of make-believe can ever fix.

CHAPTER 27

STUFF I LEARNED FROM MY (DEAD) DAUGHTER ...

When Cassidy was alive, she was truly *alive*! Now that she's gone, via that damn needle that filled her bloodstream with poison, I have found myself looking back at all the little nuggets I learned from her during her short life (much of it I learned from her death, as well). I came up with about forty-five things I learned from my only child, from her birth until today. I had to stop myself eventually, as I could have come up with forty-five more.

For those who didn't know her, she was a whirlwind of energy and wisdom. One of the most hilarious people I've ever known. Full of *life* and pain. She was truly one of a kind. Enjoy this Cassidy wisdom, from her, through me, to you. I'm pretty sure she would want all of you to learn these things, too ...

• Laugh as much as humanly possible.
• Speak your mind, even if it's unpopular.
• Don't ever be a doormat.
• Live for the moment.
• Fear nothing (even when you're scared shitless, then it's acceptable to scream like a baby).

- Follow your heart.
- Never miss an opportunity to play dress-up.
- Love like crazy.
- Fancy things make you feel special.
- Magic is real!
- Always stick up for the underdog.
- Bullies should be destroyed.
- A rich fantasy life can heal much pain.
- Sometimes it's okay to fall apart.
- Don't ever do anything half-assed.
- Food can actually make you feel better than therapy.
- Cheese should be added to everything!
- Traditions are a wonderful thing that should be respected and recreated whenever possible.
- Talking to strangers is actually fun!
- Give what you have to someone that needs it more than you.
- Snuggling is a necessity of life.
- Girl's night should never be skipped.
- Having someone to sing harmony with is never to be taken for granted.
- Music can heal a broken heart and celebrate a life all at the same time.
- When you're lost and don't know where to turn, call your mom (or dad).
- Life is seriously hard *and* it's full of wonder and love if you look in the right places.
- Watching sad movies and sobbing uncontrollably should always include milk duds and popcorn.
- Unconditional love really is possible.
- Common sense can save your life.
- If at first you don't love *Family Guy*, just keep watching till you find yourself singing the theme song out loud.
- Show tunes are to be revered and never frowned upon.
- Pedicures are not a luxury, but a necessity.
- There are two kinds of people in the world: Disney-lovers

... and dumb-dumbs.

- Always say I LOVE YOU when you have a chance, because you never know when it will be the last time.
- Don't ever pass up a fireworks show.
- Never miss an opportunity to be on stage.
- Don't be afraid to get wet when it rains. In fact, dancing in the rain is ideal.
- Pets should be your best friend. They will never judge you and will love you no matter how bizarrely you act around them.
- If you ever have an opportunity to make your parents feel uncomfortable and awkward ... TAKE IT!
- Movie quotes are always better the second and fiftieth time you say them.
- There's no such thing as taking it too far when it comes to comedy.
- Never be afraid to make a fool of yourself.
- Butterflies come straight from heaven.
- Dance like no one is watching, but secretly hope that someone is watching.
- When someone you love dies, you will never stop thinking about them.

CHAPTER 28

THE BUTTERFLY EFFECT

The butterfly effect is a part of the chaos theory that states that one small change in a situation can drastically change the outcome of an event. The circumstances which originated the term, "the butterfly effect," goes something like this: A butterfly flaps its wings in Japan, which causes tiny changes in the atmosphere, which ultimately cause a tornado to appear halfway across the world.

As I ponder the butterfly effect, I realize that I see it happening all the time, all around me, and most definitely in my own life. One tiny decision, which leads to a momentary change, that can open a new possibility, which can promote an entirely new and different outcome. I experienced it firsthand a couple weeks ago while traveling, and it's stayed with me like a lost kitten, waiting for care and feeding. So, I figure I needed to share it. Here's what happened:

I was flown out to the Milwaukee Film Festival recently for the world premiere of a film I was in called *Dear Coward on The Moon*. John and I flew out on Sunday for the screening that night, and the following evening we made our way to the Milwaukee airport to fly home to SLC, with one stop in MSP (Minneapolis). The flight from MKE to MSP was delayed upon landing, when a huge storm formed over Minneapolis. We had to remain in a holding pattern in the air for about an hour until the storm cleared so we could land. Well, as you can imagine, this created even more delays at MSP that evening. Once on the ground, we got to the gate for our flight into SLC, and they were waiting on one last flight attendant in order to start boarding. Finally, we got on the plane and settled in. As the last of the passengers were boarding the plane, one of them, a young woman (traveling alone), stopped at our row and her eyes were locked on me. She looked perplexed and engaged at the same time. I made eye contact with her and she asked, "Do I know you? I think I know you. You look so familiar."

I didn't recognize her. I asked if she lived in SLC and she said no, that she lived in St. George, Utah. I blew it off and offered, "Maybe you've seen me in a TV commercial recently?" Then she was hurried down the aisle, as those behind her were pressing her on to get to their seats.

I turned around out of curiosity once again, and she was still looking at me, her neurons firing, trying desperately to make a connection. I could see it in her eyes as she thought, "How do I know this woman?"

She then said in a slightly raised voice, so as to carry over the five or so rows between us by now, "Do you work in mental health?" she asked.

I replied, "No, but I did speak recently at a treatment center near St. George."

Ah ha!

I could see the light bulb switch on inside her, as she was once again pushed down the aisle and out of sight towards the back of the plane. At that point, I wasn't sure if she was one of the girls that heard me speak that day at Sunrise, or if she could possibly be old enough to have been one of the staff. At my age, it's hard to tell these things.

Well, the storm outside started up again and they couldn't finish loading the baggage because of lightning on the tarmac. So there we sat, waiting again.

This little added delay made this next moment possible
... The young woman makes her way back up to our row in
the front of the plane, introduced herself as Annabelle and
explained that she was there at Sunrise when I came to speak
to the girls in May. She was so touched by the story I shared
that day, my story of Cassidy, that she had been thinking about
it for a long time. She said she had just borrowed a phone to call
her mom to tell her that I was on the same flight. She hugged
me and thanked me for sharing my story with them that day
in Southern Utah. Cassidy's story had made quite an impact
on Annabelle, and she continued to share it with new girls
coming into treatment often. She explained that she had been
at Sunrise over a year now and had just been on a home visit
for two weeks in Madison, Wisconsin. She would be returning
to Sunrise tonight, after catching a connecting flight in SLC
to St. George. Apparently, she wasn't originally booked for
this flight, but they switched her at the last minute because
of possible issues with her connection in SLC. I was so glad
she introduced herself and that she had made the connection
of who I was. I was feeling like that was a huge gift, and one I
really needed at that moment. Mission accomplished! Except,
not so fast ...

After she returned to her seat and we were finally able
to take off (quite a bit later than scheduled), I couldn't stop
thinking about her. For the long three-plus-hour flight, she was
constantly on my mind. John turned to me at one point and
said, "You know, if she misses her flight, we can offer her our
guest bedroom tonight." I shrugged it off, not thinking that
far in advance. I had a whirlwind of emotions inside of me. I
couldn't stop thinking of the several home visits Cassidy had
while at Sunrise. The solo flights she took back and forth. The
worry I always felt at that time. At one point during the flight, I
went into the lavatory and sobbed for a moment. I have no idea
why. Then, I felt compelled to connect with Annabelle again
after the flight, to give her a message. The thought that kept
running through my mind was a quote from Winnie the Pooh:

"You are braver than you believe, stronger than you seem, and smarter than you think."

I grabbed the little hotel notepad from my purse and jotted down the quote, then found one of my business cards to fold inside it. I was going to hand it to her on her way off the plane. I knew she would be in a hurry to catch that next flight, and wouldn't have time to talk. But I *had* to give her this message.

As we were finally making our descent into Salt Lake, the flight attendant mentioned, with their apologies, that many connecting flights would be missed but didn't name the one to St. George, so we felt confident that Annabelle would make her connection (the last flight tonight). Upon landing, we scurried out quickly as we were up front, and when we got to the gate, we checked the monitor. The last flight to St. George had already departed!

John and I knew what we must do. We couldn't leave a sixteen-year-old girl who was in treatment for a variety of emotional issues all alone for the night, with a hotel voucher and a toiletry bag from Delta.

So we waited there until we saw her hurrying down the jet bridge. She spotted me, and as soon as she was in earshot, I said, "You missed the flight." Her lip quivered and she looked lost for a moment, as I could see the tears starting to puddle in the corner of her eyes. Then I continued, when she was standing in front of me. "... and you can stay with us, if you feel comfortable with that. We will take care of everything." She wrapped her arms around me and cried and smiled. I think I cried a little, too, if I'm being honest. Okay, yes I cried, too.

So John went on down to baggage claim as Annabelle and I went to the Delta agent to see about rebooking. They got her on the first flight in the morning, and as expected, offered her a hotel voucher, which we declined, and gave her a Delta toiletry bag with essentials since she was without her luggage for the night. As we were walking to meet up with John, I remembered I had the little note and my card that I wanted to give her, which I did. I told her to keep it and if she ever wanted to get in touch with me, that I was there for her.

On the drive to our house, I let her use my phone to call her mom so she could tell her what happened and that she was safe for the night. Apparently, while in flight, her mother had found me on Facebook and sent me a message, reaching out and asking if we could help Annabelle out in the event she missed her flight. I didn't see the message until that moment. Funny how life works. I was so grateful that we could be of help to her and put her mother's mind at ease that night. She was incredibly grateful!

As I got Annabelle settled in our guest room downstairs, she was going through the toiletry bag and handed over the razor. She told me she had struggled with cutting and didn't need that around her tonight, as it had been a very stressful day of traveling. I was so proud of her! After we checked the rest of the bathroom for sharp things, I got her something to sleep in and some fresh underwear and bid her goodnight.

As I walked upstairs to my room, I couldn't help thinking of the last time Cassidy slept in that guest room, Thanksgiving of 2014. She was visiting us from Birmingham, just after we had moved to Utah, and she happened to be withdrawing from heroin at the time. You see, Cassidy wanted to be clean when she came to visit me, but in reality her withdrawals made her almost unbearable to be around. She was angry, combative, sick, craving, and begging me to take her down to Pioneer Park so she could score some dope. While trying to decorate the Christmas tree that weekend all together, with John's two teenaged sons who lived with us, Cassidy had a moment of rage, which left us all scratching our heads and trying to act naturally at the same time. Here was my daughter, screaming at me, while cheery Christmas music played in the background, as we tried to keep smiling while pouring hot chocolate and hanging ornaments on the sparkly tree. After that visit, I told Cassidy she wasn't welcome back here if she was still using. That was the hardest thing I have ever done (next to having her burned in a crematorium, just two short years later). But I digress ... or maybe not.

The next morning, I woke Annabelle around six a.m. As she and I sat alone in the kitchen while her oatmeal was warming up, I noticed her standing by the fridge reading the laminated obituary of Cassidy's from the funeral home. I went into the office and grabbed another one (I had several), and asked if she wanted it. She was happy to accept it and thanked me. Over breakfast, she told me that she never really had a problem with substance abuse. She confided in me that she had had a lot of emotional issues: anxiety, depression, cutting, eating disorders, etc. She felt like she had made some real progress in treatment and kind of turned a corner recently. She was getting so close to graduating, and I could still see that tiny little speck of self-doubt as she talked about leaving Sunrise soon.

On our drive back to the airport, we had a wonderful talk in the car, just the two of us about my career, life, etc. She said she had been in a commercial as a child and thought about maybe acting again someday. I encouraged her to follow her passion and of course to get in touch with me if I could be of any assistance. After our goodbyes at the airport and about twenty minutes after dropping her off, I got a call from an unknown number. It was Annabelle, calling from a borrowed phone to let me know she had made it to her gate and to thank me one last time for everything I did for her!

I will never forget her and I hope she can find that thing inside her that brings her joy. That passion inside her that will lead to her purpose. She can accomplish anything she sets her mind to.

Lots of crazy circumstances brought us together on that flight, which led to a beautiful connection and an opportunity for me to help someone in need. I couldn't always help Cassidy in her lifetime, but somehow helping Annabelle that night felt like a wonderful, soothing salve on my ripped-up heart. I felt Cassidy's handprint all over this encounter. I felt like I had a little do-over for just a moment. I was and still am overwhelmed with gratitude for this opportunity that was laid out in front of me. And then I realized, it could have gone a completely different direction.

What if ...

Annabelle hadn't been rebooked on our flight? Or the flight hadn't been delayed with weather? Or she recognized me, but didn't come up to introduce herself? Or the flight to St. George hadn't been missed? Or we hadn't waited for her after the flight?

If not for these tiny moments, our evening would have turned out much differently. I think everything happened that night precisely the way it was supposed to. There are no coincidences in life. At least that's what I believe.

Thank you Cassidy for the little nudges. Thank you for sending your little butterfly effect to help out Annabelle and her parents, and, selfishly, to help me. We all needed that!

CHAPTER 29

DEAR CASSIDY,

Dear Cassidy,
It's been almost a year since you left us, and every day I ache. Every day I beat myself up for not answering that last phone call you made to me, just a few hours before you took your last breath on the bathroom floor. And even more, for not calling you back that night before I went to sleep. I'm sorry for putting it off until a tomorrow that never came for you. I am so sorry that I had to build a picket fence between us in the last few years. I missed opportunities to connect with you, and I lost out on long conversations and visits from Alabama from you.

I owe you an apology, too, for every single word I said or action I took that made it easier for you to get what you wanted from me. I know I have accountability for "helping" you sink deeper into your disease at times. I was trying so hard to make sure you were comfortable and that you still loved me, that I did everything I could to see that you stayed "happy." But really, all I accomplished was to help you remain comfortable in your bubble-wrap so you never had to feel the real consequences of the damage your disease was causing you and others ... until you did.

Cassidy, I'm sorry that I avoided you at times. I should have been honest with you and told you how your actions were affecting me, rather than pretending not to get your messages or being too busy to return a call. I am ashamed of myself for not communicating with you the way you deserved in the end. I didn't trust you.

I am so angry at you! When I think about everything we did to help you and all the resources that went into treatment and doctors and therapy! I am pissed that your damn drugs became more important to you than your family, your health, your friends, your well-being and ultimately your own life. I feel so much rage right now over every sleepless night, E.R. visit, frantic call in the middle of the night, every fight we had, every suicide threat, every drop of blood I had to clean off the floor or your clothes from self-inflicted cuts on your arms or legs. I am furious at you for lying, screaming, manipulating, stealing, blaming me. It hurt me so much.

I am so mad that any future relationship we could have had is over. It pisses me off that I won't ever be able watch you blossom and shine as a mother yourself. I feel cheated out of being right there in the birthing suite with you as you push my grandbaby into the world, all sweaty and beautiful and full of life and love. I will never have that experience with you and it makes me furious! You took that future away and it's not fair!

I think I somehow fantasized that one magical day you would suddenly be cured. You would magically be better and we could have the mother-daughter relationship we both deserved. Full of lunch dates, mutual respect, mani-pedis, honesty, holiday get-togethers, kindness, openness, mutual support, shopping, and love. (You and I never lacked in love. For that, I am eternally grateful.)

Cassidy, I also want to say thank you. Thank you for your bright light in my life for twenty-two crazy and wonderful years. Thank you for always believing in me. Thank you for pushing me to take risks and challenging my boundaries. I know I failed at times, *and* I always tried my best. *And* sometimes I was really tired and couldn't do any better. Thank you for making me laugh, and cry. Thank you for challenging my intelligence with really great questions, and thanks for always speaking your mind. I learned a lot from you. I realize it should be the other way around, but you always seemed wiser than I was. Thank you for helping me understand that the right clothes make me look good, and that I was worthy of feeling good about myself. Thank you for forcing me to get my first pedicure with you. It was life-changing. Thank you for always being willing to eat chocolate with me. And most of all, thank you for loving me back. I know you did the best you could, too, and I always knew you loved me, even in the middle of the war.

I watched a movie last night about time, the nonlinear nature of it in a parallel-universal sense. It begged the question: What if I caught a glimpse of what our life together would hold before I got pregnant with you? Would I be willing to do it all over again ... knowing the pain, the sadness, the angst, your struggles, knowing that I would lose you when you turned twenty-two, knowing that I would have to live the rest of my life spreading your ashes everywhere I went? My resounding answer is *YES*! Hell yes! I don't even need to think about that one, because I would, without hesitation, live it all over, every part of it, just to have the chance to be your mother again. The price of love is loss, and in this case, I would pay it a million times to experience the love I felt for you and from you for those short twenty-two years.

You are my sunshine, Cassidy. You were my sunshine when I held you in my arms and kissed your sweet, soft forehead as an infant, right up to the moment when I hugged your rigid shoulders and kissed your cold forehead goodbye as you lay in that wooden box. You are the one who taught me how to love, and I will be forever in your debt for that. How dare you leave me here ... but I understand why you had to go. You weren't meant for this world any longer. Fly my sweet girl. Fly and be free ... finally. It's about time you met your true potential. I am so proud of you!

All my love forever and ever, to infinity,
Mom

P.S. If you could, like, talk to me in a dream or something, that would be awesome. I miss you and could use a laugh or a hug or a smile. Life is hard without you. And Facebook isn't the same without you, either. TTFN

CHAPTER 30

A NEW NOVEMBER

My mother died at age sixty-five on 11/21/2005. Cassidy died at age twenty-two on 11/11/2016.

I have come to hate November (or so I thought), but the more I think about it, November should be a month to be celebrated. After all, November is the month when my mother and my only daughter were both finally released from the suffering they endured in their mortal bodies. It's actually a beautiful thing, the more I think about it.

Thinking back to those final months when I sat by my mother's bedside, watching her slowing being eaten away by the cancer inside her ... those are the months I should hate. June through October! The months when she would cry upon waking to find herself still alive. The months she was doubled over in excruciating pain, worried about death, angry for this plight, sobbing on my father's shoulder as he held her and told her everything would be okay through his own tears. Those months were horrific. No one should be asked to endure that kind of pain (both physical and emotional).

Although, even in those months, I managed to find the little gems, the beautiful human moments, of love, wisdom, of the ugly and gorgeous human condition. My mother had some amazing insights in those last months. I will cherish those moments forever. I am so grateful for the opportunity I had to be by her side. If she hadn't had cancer, I wouldn't have flown to Utah that often to be with my parents that year. It's a shame that it took a terminal disease with a timeline to force that connection. I was able to say everything I needed to say to her before she died. I was lucky enough to soothe her when she wept, to lay next to her as she slept, and stroke her hair when she cried. Not everyone gets those opportunities. And I thank God every single day for that.

As I type this, I start to get angry that I didn't get that same opportunity with Cassidy. I didn't get to stroke her hair until she lay motionless in a wooden box. Yet, there I sat all that time, fully knowing Cassidy suffered from a terminal disease that could take her life at any moment ... yet, I created boundaries to protect myself, I didn't return phone calls, I was afraid to answer the phone for fear of the drama on the other end. I secretly wished for all the craziness to be over, yet I wasn't ready for the reality of that wish.

Well ... I got my "wish."

The craziness is over now. No more drama, no more middle-of-the-night phone calls asking for bail money, no more texts loaded with manipulation, no more screaming and blaming. No more holiday visits or Facebook messages. No more sweet birthday wishes or phones calls to wish me Happy Mother's Day! No more pedicures together or fondue and movie nights. No more hugs and no more silly pictures together. No more vacations to the beach or Disney World. It's all over now.

Here I now sit, today, on this, the anniversary of my mother's death, just ten days following the anniversary of Cassidy's death.

A New November. One which I reclaim now. No longer shall November be a month of despair, sadness, and grief. Instead I choose to celebrate November. An astounding and beautiful thing happened in November ... Two kind, happy, tortured, beautiful women, who happened to mean the world to me, were finally set free. The woman who was the first to love me unconditionally and the girl who would love me unconditionally as only a child could. They were finally allowed to leave all the suffering behind them and transform into the most amazing version of themselves. No more cancer, no more addiction, no more pain, no more sadness or turmoil. Only flight, light, love, and the most amazing joy!

Happy November, Mom and Cassidy. I love you, and I know you both really understand just how much now.

My Mom and Cassidy in New York City, 2005

CHAPTER 31

IT IS OKAY TO BE OKAY ...

"It is okay to be okay."

These were Cassidy's words in a dream that her dad had shortly after her death. Her message to me was, *"Tell Mom it is okay to be okay, we've all suffered enough already."*

Well, it took me awhile, but I'm ready to hear that message now, and even more importantly, I am ready to live it. I'm pretty sure this will be my final chapter here. You see, I am graduating! Make no mistake, that doesn't mean I'm done grieving or that I am magically all better. Let me try to explain ... I've come a long way since November 11, 2016. This time last year I was still in a state of shock. I didn't realize it at the time, but looking back at myself in the news stories and Facebook posts from the past year, it's clear that I was just on autopilot, floating through space, through no will or power of my own. Thank God for that.

Speaking of God, for those that know me well, I am not much the praying type, at least not in the traditional sense. I have always believed in a force of love, a creator, a higher universal power ... *Okay*, so I pretty much believe in God! Since Cassidy died, I have found myself, on many occasions, conversing out loud with this higher power. Usually I find myself talking to

God on my evening walks with Zoey (our amazingly intuitive Golden-doodle). This has become my therapeutic magic hour of sorts.

Just a couple weeks ago, following the first anniversary of Cassidy's death, I had a life-changing moment on our walk. First I was talking to Cassidy, asking her to tell me she was okay. I was pleading actually, the tears rolling down my face. Begging for some sign from her, a way to know she still existed in some form! Moments later ... I was hit with an overwhelming sense of peace and warmth. I felt it right down to my core, and the tears suddenly changed from those of anguish and uncertainty, to tears of beauty and gratitude. That lump in my throat and the pain in my chest disappeared, and what I was left with was this intense calm. The tears kept steadily flowing, but they were now tears as clear as crystal, full of love and understanding and sheer joy. I have never felt anything like it before. At that moment, in the middle of the street in the neighborhood behind our house, I *knew*! I knew Cassidy was at peace, that she is still part of this universe and that she is happy, content and in the presence of the purest love and brightest light imaginable. I felt her there with me and I knew she was *happy*. I have never felt that kind of love in my life. It was absolutely euphoric!

I then started talking to God, water flowing from my eyes, but really coming from my soul. I said out loud how grateful I was and thanked God for this beautiful gift. Then, I uttered the words I never thought I would say in a million years. I looked out into the vast universe and I said, "God, thank you for taking Cassidy back to be with you, thank you for setting her free from her suffering. I am so grateful that she is allowed to feel pure love, joy and peace, THANK YOU ..."

So there I stood, thanking God for letting Cassidy die! It was surreal and beautiful and bizarre. And since that day, I have felt a shift in me. It's been a little easier to smile, to get out of bed, to connect and stay present with others. I am noticing that I am feeling more fully (including the sadness). I am ready for stronger emotions now with the knowledge that I will survive them. You see, I was given this gift and I am making the choice to *accept* it. I've known all along the key to a happy life is *acceptance*, radical acceptance for what life gives us. We don't have to be happy about life's challenges or losses; perhaps just to be content is enough. After all, there's certainly nothing I can do to change it.

So, that's my story ... so far. I am not finished grieving. I never will be. I will continue to evolve, and I refuse to ever get stuck in the muck. I will continue to give myself permission to be okay. Being okay doesn't take away the love I have for Cassidy. We don't have to marinate in sadness or spend our lives in agony for our losses. That does nothing to prove how much we loved our children. I know we all have our own path and our journey of grief is a very individual ride. For me, I choose to give myself permission (although I really got permission from Cassidy). I decided to learn a thing or two from my angel daughter. After all, she does have a better perspective now. A high price to pay for eternal wisdom and pure unconditional love.

I can almost hear Cassidy's voice, telling me it's okay ...

"Mom, it is okay to laugh, to succeed, to love. It's okay to have fun, to play, to explore, to travel, to be a family. It's okay to sing in the car, to make jokes, to hug Zoey. It's okay to talk about me, to tell stories, to be heard. It is okay to live happily ever after and to be a grandmother one day.

"It is okay to be okay! We've all suffered enough already. The time to heal is now, and this now has never existed before. Embrace it and breathe it in." - Cassidy Aspen Cochran

EPILOGUE

So, believe it or not, my grief journey didn't end after chapter 31. I still occasionally find myself in the grocery store or an elevator, fighting back tears so as not to embarrass myself in public. It is usually brought on by a song, or sometimes just a thought of her smile, or the fact that her adorable two-year-old self used to call elevators, "eloweenings." When these moments happen to me while I'm driving (the ugly snot-crying on the freeway), I can't help but remember living as an actor in L.A. and the fact that seeing people crying or screaming while driving was just another day in La-La Land, where actors were always rehearsing their scenes on the way to auditions. Not unusual. However, when you are in Utah crying in your car, people tend to notice and feel concern.

Since Cassidy's death, I have sought out opportunities to scatter her ashes in various locations that had meaning to her, or simply places she never had the chance to visit in her short life. To date, her "carbon footprint" has found its way to: a beautiful beach on the Pacific Ocean near Santa Barbara, the Gulf Coast in Florida in Sandestin (a favorite family vacation spot), just off the Golden Gate Bridge, the Japanese Tea Gardens in San Francisco, a summit near Park City near where Cassidy loved to snowboard, a peaceful spot in the red rocks of Southern Utah, near the residential treatment center where she spent her junior year, at her grandmother's grave in Logan, Utah and finally at the Triund Temple at the top of the Himalayas in India. My intention is to continue this mission until most of my portion of her is given back to the earth. Some other places are still on the agenda because she loved them or always wanted to go: Africa, Angel's Landing at

Zion National Park, Disney World, The Wizarding World of Harry Potter, New York City, Paris, her favorite ski resorts in Canada ...

I know I will continue to find the perfect places to lay her to rest as the years go by. I truly believe that experiences, more than objects, will stay with us in our soul beyond what we know now. In life, I wanted to give Cassidy experiences that would enlighten her, bring her joy, and connect us to each other. She had so many of those in her lifetime, but the ones we didn't get to because time wasn't on her side, well, those are what I can give her now. And more importantly now, those experiences are what I can give to myself, as long as I'm living.

So, my journey continues ... through tears, laughter, nightmares, dreams, ambition, love, carrying a bit of my daughter in a plastic bag in my purse (just in case I find the perfect place to throw her to the wind). Ultimately, my life is one of openness. I am grateful for the chance to share my story.

Someone will find my story that needs it, and that's enough. I loved, I lost. Many others are in the same boat. Let's throw on a life jacket and paddle the rapids together, knowing that sometimes the water calms itself and allows for floating. Thank God! We only get pulled under when we fight too vigorously or we just give up. My new normal is trying to find the balance. The grand tight rope act of life! I'm doing okay today ... and really, that's all I have.

ABOUT THE AUTHOR

Charla Bocchicchio is an actress and acting coach, appearing in films, TV and commercials, both locally and nationally. She started writing a blog about her own journey of grief in 2016, after she lost her only child, 22 year old Cassidy, to a fentanyl overdose. Through that blog, she began to find her voice as a grieving mother that would one day be okay and eventually help others by bringing into the light what many were going through in the dark corners of their own minds. Charla now speaks at treatment centers and high schools to spread awareness about Substance Use Disorder, bringing a message of love, acceptance and non-judgment. She truly believes this is the only way to fight the disease: to stop the stigma surrounding it so that one day seeking appropriate and effective treatment for SUD is as normal and accepted as getting treatment for diabetes or cancer. Charla is married to a wonderful, supportive man, John. He has always believed in her and held her up. And without his love, she wouldn't know how to function in the world any longer. They live in Salt Lake City, UT with their amazingly intuitive Golden doodle, Zoey. In her spare time, Charla can be found in the yoga studio.

Made in the USA
San Bernardino, CA
14 December 2019

61498217R00078